Key Topics in Political Psychology

This highly accessible book provides an overview of the discipline of political psychology. It breaks down political psychology into five key areas that discuss the history, impact, and future directions of the subject. This book covers the origins of the discipline, an overview of the most important theories in political psychology, a discussion of methodology, how political psychology is applied in practice in terms of policy, as well as a discussion of the emerging areas in political psychology research.

It captures the state of the art in the discipline, introducing students to political psychology and how it can help address major societal challenges. Importantly, this book describes how political psychology can be applied in policymaking, enhancing readers' opportunities to apply its empirical and analytical material across a range of global contexts.

Providing a handy introduction to political psychology, this book will be essential reading for undergraduate and postgraduate students of political psychology, social psychology, and political behavior. It will also be a useful reference point for students and a teaching resource for lecturers in the field of political communication.

Pavlos Vasilopoulos is Senior Lecturer at the Department of Politics and International Relations at the University of York and Associate Researcher at the Center for Political Research (CEVIPOF) at Sciences Po, Paris.

BPS Key Topics in Psychology

British Psychological Society

Routledge, in partnership with the British Psychological Society (BPS), is pleased to present *BPS Key Topics in Psychology*, a series of short introductory books that focus on a specific field within psychology. Each book is broken down into bitesize chunks to provide a helpful overview of core psychology topics, made clear by a five-part structure: foundations, theories, methodologies, impacts, and emerging areas. Written by active and experienced authors, these essential books encourage students to approach fundamental concepts with confidence and critical thinking.

Books may incorporate student-friendly pedagogies, including tools such as: feature boxes; key terms and definitions; and links to further reading online. Concise yet comprehensive, these books offer a simple and accessible overview of core psychology topics for students looking for a summary of key concepts in the topic, or those new to the area.

Key Topics in Counselling Psychology
Terry Hanley and Laura Anne Winter

Key Topics in Clinical Neuropsychology
Sara da Silva Ramos, Dr. Christopher Byrne and Rudi Coetzer

Key Topics in Memory
Richard J. Allen and Charity Brown

Key Topics in Parenting and Family Psychology
Alina Morawska & Amy E. Mitchell

Key Topics in Identity Development
Theo A. Klimstra

Key Topics in Political Psychology
Pavlos Vasilopoulos

For more information about this series, please visit: www.routledge.com/BPS-Key-Topics-in-Psychology/book-series/BPSKTP

Key Topics in Political Psychology

Pavlos Vasilopoulos

Routledge
Taylor & Francis Group
LONDON AND NEW YORK

Designed cover image: Paul Henry Lysaker

First published 2027
by Routledge
4 Park Square, Milton Park, Abingdon, Oxon OX14 4RN

and by Routledge
605 Third Avenue, New York, NY 10158

Routledge is an imprint of the Taylor & Francis Group, an informa business

British Library Cataloguing-in-Publication Data
A catalogue record for this book is available from the British Library

ISBN: 9781032606682 (hbk)
ISBN: 9781032606675 (pbk)
ISBN: 9781003460084 (ebk)

DOI: 10.4324/9781003460084

Typeset in Galliard
by codeMantra

Access the Support Material: www.routledge.com/9781032606675

To my parner, Haley and my daughter, Vera.

To George E. Marcus, for his mentoring, kindness, and support throughout my career.

Contents

Contents

To my parner, Haley and my daughter, Vera.

To George E. Marcus, for his mentoring, kindness, and support throughout my career.

Acknowledgments

First and foremost, I would like to thank my partner, Haley McAvay, for her love and constant encouragement throughout the course of this project. Her belief in the value of this book and her constructive and meticulous feedback were indispensable to its completion.

I would also like to express my gratitude to my friends Viki Antonopoulou, Neil Carter, Penelope Dimitrakopoulou, Saba Joshi, Markos Katsimis, Jeremy Moulton, and Justin Robinson for being there for me – whether listening stoically about political psychology or bearing with me with updates about how the work was (or was not) progressing. I would also like to warmly thank my colleagues Gabriele Badano, Monica Brito-Viera, Jeremy Moulton, Alasia Nuti, and Sofia Stathi for their excellent feedback on earlier drafts of the chapters.

Finally, I am deeply grateful to my former and current students both at Sciences Po and at the University of York. Their curiosity, commitment, and enthusiasm make teaching Political Psychology such a rewarding and fulfilling endeavor. I wrote this book with them in mind, and I sincerely hope it can ignite a spark in some of its readers to engage more deeply with this fascinating academic field.

Section 1

Key Foundations

Chapter 1

What Is Political Psychology?

What Is Political Psychology?

Political psychology: The application of psychological science to the study of political behavior.

Political psychology is often described as the scientific offspring of the marriage between political science and psychology (Deutsch & Kinvall, 2008). At its simplest conception, it refers to "the study of mental processes that underlie political judgments and decision making" (Kuklinski, 2002, p. 2), or "an application of what is known about human psychology to the study of politics" (Sears et al., 2003, p. 3).

Political psychology definitions are broad, perhaps frustratingly so. This is because political psychologists do not adhere to a common set of scientific assumptions. In fact, interdisciplinarity and pluralism lie at the core of political psychology. This has been the case since its conceptual birth and continues to be so until this day. The diversity includes theoretical standpoints, approaches, methods, and, as with any scientific discipline, conclusions. For this reason, some scholars contend that it is more accurate to refer to "political psychologies" rather than a single political psychology, since the latter would imply the existence of a set of common scientific foundations or a shared scientific object (Sears et al., 2003). While psychology and political science lie at the core of the discipline, political psychology also employs theoretical tools and methodological approaches from sociology, economics, anthropology, and, more recently, biology and **neuroscience**. Trying to capture this interdisciplinarity, Elad-Strenger and Mintz (2015) posit that

Neuroscience: A scientific discipline studying the nervous system with a focus on the structure and function of the brain.

DOI: 10.4324/9781003460084-2

> research in political psychology aims at understanding, explaining, and predicting the effects of psychological dynamics, political structures, and political processes in broad social and historical contexts on political behaviour, political decision-making, **intergroup** and **intragroup relations** and other political phenomena such as elections, political protest, violence, conflict, and terrorism.
>
> (p. 1)

What becomes immediately apparent from any definition of political psychology is its bidirectional nature. As Deutsch and Kinvall put it, "Perceptions, beliefs, motives, and values influence political behavior at the same time as cultural and structural factors have an impact on who we are" (Deutsch & Kinvall, 2008, p. 33). In this view, political psychology seeks both to understand the psychological underpinnings of our political choices and to understand how political processes affect the self. At the same time, it is true that the pathway from psychology to politics is much more dominant in political psychology research than the pathway from politics to psychological processes. This has led prominent political psychologists Jon Krosnick and Kathleen McGraw to describe political psychology as "psychological political science", meaning that it is mostly psychology that contributes to our understanding of politics rather than the other way around (Krosnick & McGraw, 2008). Yet there are some notable exceptions where the studies of the role of psychology in political processes give birth to findings that refine or extend psychological theories. This holds particularly true in today's polarized political environment where people are increasingly sorted into different ideological camps on the basis of their **cognitive styles** and psychological structures (e.g., Hetherington & Weiler, 2018). One example where the psychological study of politics is useful for psychology is recent research on misinformation. Studies show that many people do not update their beliefs and political preferences even after having encountered – and even accepted – evidence that these beliefs are misinformed (Thorson, 2016). This paradoxical finding has helped to advance knowledge on how human memory works (Ecker et al., 2022). Another example is a recent study showing that political partisanship

Intergroup relations: The relations between members of two or more different social groups.

Intragroup relations: The relations between members of the same social group.

Cognitive style: A person's dispositional manner of thinking, learning, and processing information.

may alter one's personality traits as a result of people adopting the worldviews and behaviors of their politically like-minded peers (Bakker et al., 2021).

Political psychology is characterized by a plethora of research themes and scientific objects. Personality and political choice, the psychological motivations of prejudice, the dynamics of intergroup and intragroup relations, the psychology of **social norms**, the development of social and political identities, stereotyping, political information processing, the role of emotions in political decision-making, the impact of threat on political attitudes, and the role of socialization in political behavior are all key research objects in political psychology. But even this broad range of objects is perhaps too narrow to capture the breadth and depth of the discipline. For instance, political psychology can also extend to the elite level, that is, it aims at employing psychological theories to explain how politicians reach political decisions (see Sheffer et al., 2018).

Social norms: Informal rules of what behavior is acceptable or unacceptable in society.

The Organization of Political Psychology

Even though we can trace some key themes of political psychology back to the beginnings of Western philosophy, there was no systematic analysis of the psychological drivers of political action until the 1940s and 1950s. Scholars in post-war societies sought to understand the psychological mechanisms involved in the atrocities committed by Nazi Germany in the Second World War as well as address contemporary societal challenges. In the 1970s, a number of US universities started joint programs in psychology and politics (Elad-Strenger & Mintz, 2015). A major milestone in the institutionalization of the field was the launch of the *International Society of Political Psychology (ISPP)* in 1978. The aim of the ISPP is "to establish a community of scholars and concerned individuals in universities, government, the communications media, and elsewhere, who have scientific and practical interests in examining the relationship between political and psychological phenomena".[1] It now has more than 800 members from 70 countries (Pratto, 2024). *Political Psychology*, the flagship journal of the discipline, was established in 1980 and quickly became one of the internationally leading journals in psychology and political science in terms of readership and academic impact. The growing recognition of political psychology as an established academic field is further underlined by the increasing number of political psychology modules offered in universities across the world. Finally, as discussed in detail in Chapter 10, political psychology research often comes with practical implications for politics.

At the same time, political psychology, like many other academic disciplines, has been overly focused on Western, Educated, Industrialized, Rich, and Democratic (W.E.I.R.D.) populations. The foundations of modern political psychology have been mostly developed in the United States, with Europe being a distant second when it comes to the number of research programs, research centers, and academic publications. The Western-centrism of the discipline represents a significant limitation. It is not only a matter of social justice concerning inequality in scientific development between privileged and unprivileged countries or social groups but is also a considerable drawback that impoverishes the field as a whole. Considering the association between psychological processes and political outcomes found in the WEIRD populations as *universal* provides the false impression that findings from W.E.I.R.D countries will replicate across different populations. This may lead to an overgeneralization of research findings and conclusions that undermines the scientific validity and the academic mission of the field (Pratto, 2024). Further, the Western-centric nature of political psychological research comes with implicit assumptions of what is interesting or uninteresting, appropriate or inappropriate, desirable or undesirable as an object of study (Pratto, 2024).

Recently, there has been increased awareness of the drawbacks of a Western-focused political psychology. This has led to a rich and productive stream of research programs. Some scholars investigate the extent to which established political psychology hypotheses can be confirmed in non-Western settings (e.g., Alper & Yilmaz, 2019; Bartusevičius et al., 2020; Beattie et al., 2022; Erisen, 2024; Fatke, 2017). For example, Beattie et al. investigated whether the same established links between individual psychological traits (such as threat sensitivity or dogmatism) and political ideology in the West can be found in China (2022). Their findings showed that psychological traits mostly associated with being conservative in the West are more strongly associated with being left-wing in the Chinese setting. Others look into whether key psychometric scales used in political psychology are interpreted in the same way among ethnic majority and minority populations (Pérez & Hetherington, 2014). Finally, a third stream of study explores the extent to which established associations in political psychology apply to ethnic minorities within W.E.I.R.D countries (Philpot & White, 2010; Phoenix, 2019; Vitriol et al., 2020). All of these research programs suggest that the association between mental processes and political judgments is often conditional on the culture, history, and norms of different nations.

The Evolution of Political Psychology

As is the case with any scientific discipline, political psychology evolves. This evolution is driven by theoretical and methodological innovations that lead to the refinement of established theories and the production of more robust research. For instance, the first waves of political psychology research in the late 1940s and early 1950s relied heavily on **psychoanalysis** (e.g., Lasswell, 2016; Adorno et al., 1950). Today, studies drawing on psychoanalysis are

Psychoanalysis: A psychological theoretical and methodological tradition that focuses on the exploration of the unconscious mind and the way it affects consciousness and behavior.

rather rare, having been marginalized in psychological research and replaced with contemporary psychological approaches such as cognitive or behavioral theories (Marcus, 2012). Similarly, more contemporary political psychology has been shaped by a rich stream of research that draws on theoretical and methodological advancements in modern neuroscience (e.g., Jost et al., 2014; Zmigrod & Tsakiris, 2021). The reasons behind the constant evolution of political psychology are not however limited to the need for ever-improving scientific rigor. They also stem from societal transformation and new political challenges that have become the focus of attention for political psychologists: The resurgence of the radical right, democratic backsliding, the dehumanization of refugees and minority ethnic groups, science denialism, and the proliferation of misinformation.

Overview of This Book

This textbook aims to provide accessible reviews of at least some of the central themes of the discipline. It is of course impossible to even aspire to capture the entirety of the research areas and findings. As I hope to convey in the rest of this book, political psychology research offers intriguing insights on the psychological underpinnings of our political behavior and decision-making processes. In the following chapter, I discuss the roots of contemporary political psychological thought in the recount of an intellectual journey that finds its roots in ancient Greek philosophy. The second part of this book delves into key political psychology theories. I start by offering an overview of exciting research on the association between our personality traits as well as other long-term individual differences (such as authoritarianism or social dominance orientation) and our political choices (Chapters 3 and 4). Chapter 5 discusses how social influence shapes our perception and political behavior, while Chapter 6 investigates the psychology of intergroup relations and the psychological underpinnings of prejudice. The next chapter focuses on how citizens process political information and reach political decisions even in the absence of it (Chapter 7). Chapter 8 provides an overview of the role of emotions on political decision-making processes. Part 3 of this book is devoted to some of the key methods for studying political psychology, providing an overview of both quantitative and qualitative approaches. Part 4 is concerned with practical applications of political psychology in policy-making, political campaigns, and fighting misinformation around issues such as climate change. Finally, this book concludes with a discussion of the new trends and directions in political psychological research that will shape the field in the following years.

Further Reading

https://ispp.org/: The website of the International Society of Political Psychology.
https://www.fourbeers.com/25: An episode of the popular podcast Two Psychologists, Four Beers, discussing political psychology with Prof. John T. Jost.

Note

1 ISPP Website https://ispp.org/about/.

References

Adorno, T. W., Frenkel-Brunswik, E., Levinson, D. J., & Sanford, R. N. (1950). *The authoritarian personality*. New York: Harper and Row.

Alper, S., & Yilmaz, O. (2019). How is the Big Five related to moral and political convictions: The moderating role of the WEIRDness of the culture. *Personality and Individual Differences*, *145*, 32–38.

Bakker, B. N., Lelkes, Y., & Malka, A. (2021). Reconsidering the link between self-reported personality traits and political preferences. *American Political Science Review*, *115* (4), 1482–1498.

Bartusevičius, H., van Leeuwen, F., & Petersen, M. B. (2020). Dominance-driven autocratic political orientations predict political violence in Western, educated, industrialized, rich, and democratic (WEIRD) and non-WEIRD samples. *Psychological Science*, *31* (12), 1511–1530.

Beattie, P., Chen, R., & Bettache, K. (2022). When left is right and right is left: The psychological correlates of political ideology in China. *Political Psychology*, *43* (3), 457–488.

Deutsch, M., & Kinvall, C. (2008). What is political psychology? In K. R. Monroe (Ed.), *political psychology* (pp. 15–42). London: Routledge.

Ecker, U. K., Lewandowsky, S., Cook, J., Schmid, P., Fazio, L. K., Brashier, N., … & Amazeen, M. A. (2022). The psychological drivers of misinformation belief and its resistance to correction. *Nature Reviews Psychology*, *1* (1), 13–29.

Elad-Strenger, J., & Mintz, A. (2015). Political psychology. In G. Mazzoleni (Ed.), *The international encyclopaedia of political communication* (pp. 1–10). Hoboken, NJ: John Wiley & Sons.

Erisen, C. (2024). Emotional predictors of populism in the case of Turkey. *American Behavioral Scientist*, *69* (14), 1687–1710.

Fatke, M. (2017). Personality traits and political ideology: A first global assessment. *Political Psychology*, *38* (5), 881–899.

Hetherington, M., & Weiler, J. (2018). *Prius or pickup?: How the answers to four simple questions explain America's great divide*. Boston: Houghton Mifflin.

Jost, J. T., Nam, H. H., Amodio, D. M., & Van Bavel, J. J. (2014). Political neuroscience: The beginning of a beautiful friendship. *Political Psychology*, *35*, 3–42.

Krosnick, J., & McGraw, K. (2008). Psychological political science versus political psychology true to its name: A plea for balance. In K. R. Monroe (Ed.), *Political psychology* (pp. 79–94). London: Routledge.

Kuklinski, J. H. (2002). *Thinking about political psychology*. Cambridge: Cambridge University Press.

Lasswell, H. D. (2016). *Psychopathology and Politics.* Chicago: University of Chicago Press. (Original work published 1930).
Marcus, G. E. (2012). *Political psychology: Neuroscience, genetics, and politics.* Oxford: Oxford University Press.
Nesbitt-Larking, P., & Kinnvall, C. (2012). The discursive frames of political psychology. *Political Psychology, 33* (1), 45–59.
Pérez, E. O., & Hetherington, M. J. (2014). Authoritarianism in black and white: Testing the cross-racial validity of the child rearing scale. *Political Analysis, 22* (3), 398–412.
Philpot, T., & White, I. (Eds.). (2010). *African-American political psychology: Identity, opinion, and action in the post-civil rights era.* London: Springer.
Phoenix, D. L. (2019). *The anger gap: How race shapes emotion in politics.* Cambridge University Press: Cambridge.
Pratto, F. (2024). ISPP presidential address: Why political psychology (and ISPP) benefit from including work (and members) from varieties of political systems, positions and locations, political cultures, theories, and methods. *Political Psychology, 45,* 437–453.
Sears, D. O., Huddy, L., & Jervis, R. (2003). The psychologies underlying political psychology. In D. O. Sears, L. Huddy, & R. Jervis (Eds.), *Oxford handbook of political psychology* (pp. 3–16). Oxford: Oxford University Press.
Sheffer, L., Loewen, P. J., Soroka, S., Walgrave, S., & Sheafer, T. (2018). Nonrepresentative representatives: An experimental study of the decision making of elected politicians. *American Political Science Review, 112* (2), 302–321.
Thorson, E. (2016). Belief echoes: The persistent effects of corrected misinformation. *Political Communication, 33* (3), 460–480.
Vitriol, J. A., Larsen, E. G., & Ludeke, S. G. (2020). Just as WEIRD? Personality traits and political attitudes among immigrant minorities. *Journal of Research in Personality, 85,* 103931.
Zmigrod, L., & Tsakiris, M. (2021). Computational and neurocognitive approaches to the political brain: Key insights and future avenues for political neuroscience. *Philosophical Transactions of the Royal Society B, 376* (1822), 20200130.

Chapter 2

The Foundations of Contemporary Political Psychology

Introduction

The chief aim of the discipline of political psychology is to understand political behavior using theoretical tools from psychological science. Political psychologists ultimately seek to explain individual preferences regarding the political organization of a community and the goals of collective action. The organization of humans into societies and the problems associated with ruling and collective decision-making inevitably place psychology at the center of the study of politics. As George Marcus, a prominent political psychologist, states:

> For a very long time, humans have inquired about their nature, seeking to reconcile their political beliefs and aspirations with what they took to be their underlying essence. It has been a common presumption that whatever this essence is, and however it might be stretched by growth or stunned by deprivation, we must begin with a sound understanding of human psychology.
>
> (2001, p. 95)

In this sense, traces of what we now call political psychology have been implicitly or explicitly present in much of classical and early modern political philosophy.

It is important to remember that unlike modern political psychologists who employ specific psychological theories to understand political choices, philosophers were rather concerned with constructing "psychologies with political intent" (Neblo, 2007, p. 26). In other words, in classical and early modern political philosophy "a philosopher's descriptive psychology had to serve as a logical base for his moral psychology, which served, in turn, to underwrite his ethical theory, and on to his political theory" (Neblo, 2007, p. 26). The list of such works is extensive, making it impossible to cover them all in one textbook chapter. Nonetheless, some key works stand out and are considered

DOI: 10.4324/9781003460084-3

foundational. This chapter aims to offer a concise overview of the philosophical origins of political psychology as well as to describe the foundations of modern political psychology.

The Early Origins of Political Psychology

The association between human nature and governance is perhaps most evident in classical Greek philosophy. The nature of citizen participation in city-states and the discussion of the qualities of optimal political regimes constitute central themes in classical Greek philosophy, touching on questions that could be considered political psychological in a broad sense: the nature of the soul, the fundamental needs of human nature, the basis of morality, the relation between reason and emotion, the right form of government, and the meaning and structure of the good society. In the *Republic*, Plato examines how soul and city, ethics and politics, shape each other (2012). He connects the characteristics of different types of communities with the personalities of the individuals that comprise them, as "the elements and traits that belong to a state must also exist in the individuals that compose it" (435e). The soul-city connection echoes themes in contemporary political psychology discussing individual differences in support for different forms of governance and political outcomes.

On the other hand, Plato's student and critic Aristotle developed a theory of political naturalism (1998). He famously described man as a "political animal", who stands out from other animals because of language. Language, according to Aristotle, enables men to deliberate about how to act, that is "serves to declare what is advantageous and what is the reverse, and it is the peculiarity of man, in comparison with other animals, that he alone possesses a perception of good and evil, of the just and the unjust" (1253a7). The human capacity for speech and moral reasoning provides the basis for the "natural impulse" of men to organize politically within the context of the city-state. More than a millennium later, English political philosopher Thomas Hobbes engaged with proto-psychological traits in his major work *Leviathan* (1996) to discuss human nature, yet painting a markedly different picture compared to Aristotle. The English philosopher argued that man is naturally unsociable and argued that man's natural state is violence, war, and an endless conflict over limited natural resources. Speech for Hobbes, and especially moral language, is a major source of conflict among men. He foregrounds three main causes of conflict responsible for making the condition of war natural to man: competition, diffidence, and glory. Conflict will ensue because while some people might compete for gain, others will try to conquer for reputation, with the impending possibility of aggression incentivizing preemptive first strikes. Life in the absence of an established political order is thus "solitary, poor, nasty, brutish, and short". What makes government and the law feasible is not the striving for virtue but the fear of death that comes with living in a state of nature: "The original of all great, and lasting societies, consisted not in the mutual good will men had toward each other, but in the mutual fear they had of each other" (Hobbes, 1998, p. 8). Hobbes' philosophy places fear as the central motivating force behind the formation and maintenance of society and political organization. It echoes modern political psychology where the role of emotions, and fear in particular, in collective action, ideology, and political participation is a major research focus (e.g., Jost et al., 2017; Marcus et al., 2000).

Niccolo Machiavelli's *The Prince* is another work that is considered influential in the development of modern political psychology. In this 16th-century treatise on effective rule-making, Machiavelli uses a theory of "humors" (a term he uses interchangeably with "desire" and "appetite") in determining the form of regime. He associates different humors with different groups (namely, the great and the people), and the form of regime depends ultimately upon the balance of the humors, the degree to which one humor dominates the other, and the degree to which humors are corrupted. *The Prince* offers a rather dark and cynical view of human nature, promoting a leadership style based on ruthlessness, oppression, and deception. With the aim of describing the traits of effective leadership, Machiavelli touches on many themes that formed key research topics in political psychology several centuries later. These include the conditions of accepting or rejecting authority, the formation of political impressions, as well as the role of love and fear in supporting effective leadership (Machiavelli, 2021). Also, like Hobbes, Machiavelli presented fear *and* hope as two equally foundational, complementary passions, for the maintenance of political orders, whether republics or principalities.

A further notable work touching on core themes found in contemporary political psychology is Gustav Le Bon's *The Crowd* (1960), one of the earliest treatises on mass behavior. Le Bon's conception of the crowd reflected his own experience as an observer of the emergence of radical social movements in late 19th-century France, particularly the Paris Commune, a short-lived revolutionary socialist government. Le Bon famously argued that individuals, when amassed in crowds, lose their individual qualities. The replacement of individual identity by a collective mindset results in the lifting of rational self-controls and the adoption of extreme behaviors uncharacteristic of an individual. Through submergence in a crowd, individuals see themselves united by a fundamentally emotional experience, which makes them think, feel, and act the same way as the crowd, and give in to the most primitive instincts. This loss of individuality and normal control mechanisms makes them vulnerable to propaganda and manipulation. In the crowd, he writes that "the conscious personality has entirely vanished; will and discernment are lost. All feelings and thought are bent in the direction determined by the hypnotiser" (p. 18). Despite relying on what we would consider today to be pseudoscientific principles, Le Bon's work was particularly pioneering as he investigated the psychological underpinnings of mass behavior. The psychological processes covered in this book are remarkably similar to the ones that contemporary political psychology engages with, such as emotions and political action, information processing, or attitude formation and change.

Of equal significance in the development of modern political psychology was the publication of *Human Nature in Politics* by Graham Wallas (1908). Wallas, a pioneering social psychologist and one of the founders of the London School of Economics, took issue with what he called "intellectualist fallacy": the idea that political and economic decision-making rests exclusively on a reasoned, rational calculus of the optimal means to arrive at a preconceived end, which is usually defined by self-interest. This view dominated early social science at the beginning of the 20th century and is still popular among some politicians, journalists, and pundits. Wallas argued that this was a rather naïve conception of political action that neglected the role of "human nature". Instead, he argued that people "act in politics under the immediate stimulus of affection and instinct" (1908, p. 53). That is, political thought and action have little to do with conscious self-interest but are instead guided by habits, impulses, emotions, and unconscious processes that are inaccessible to the conscious self. Wallas believed that bringing psychology to the study of politics would be necessary to truly understand political action. Traces of Wallas' thought can be found in several research streams of modern political psychology, especially when it comes to information processing and the role of emotions in decision-making.

The Foundations of Contemporary Political Psychology

So far we have traced the conceptual foundations of modern political psychology in early European philosophical thought. Contemporary political psychology, however, was developed predominantly in the United States. Despite the wealth of theoretical and methodological approaches that characterize the field, political psychologists identify five broad time periods, each of which had a different theoretical and methodological focus concerning the interplay of psychology and political behavior (McGuire, 1993; Sullivan et al., 2002). In this section I provide an overview of each.

Most scholars agree that the foundations of modern political psychology are set during and in the immediate aftermath of the Second World War (Sullivan et al., 2002). In its infancy, the discipline was heavily **psychoanalytic**, drawing particularly on Freudian theory to understand political behavior. The overarching theme was the

Psychoanalysis: A psychological theoretical and methodological tradition that focuses on the exploration of the unconscious mind and the way it affects consciousness and behavior.

revelation of the "irrational" motives of political action (e.g., Lasswell, 2016). This irrationality referred to the latent and often unrecognized desires and affective drives originating from an individual's private life, particularly their early childhood. These were thought to leave a lasting mark on personality. A seminal example of research from this era included the study of the psychology of politically active people by Harold Lasswell (2016). Lasswell highlighted the role of developmental experiences in shaping political interest and different types of political action, arguing that political action is the reflection of private, unconscious affects onto political objects. Other ground-breaking works during the same period focused on the development of personality and its association with political ideology. A prominent example is *The Authoritarian Personality* by Adorno et al. (1950), who described authoritarianism as a product of early child socialization within the context of the family (Adorno et al., 1950, see also Chapter 3 in this book). In summary, early political psychologists were interested in acquiring an overview of life histories and latent desires that shape personality and, in turn, political action, ideology, and political choice. Methodologically, what is now considered the first era of modern political psychological research involved in-depth psychotherapy sessions and the examination of clinical files.

The psychoanalytical approach to political psychology started to lose ground during the 1950s and especially during the 1960s in favor of a behavioral turn. This transition was first and foremost grounded in a methodological evolution. Following advances in **sampling methods** and the development of **psychometric scales**, the state of the art in research methods switched from psychobiography, and the pursuit of the discovery of the role of unconscious impulses, to quantitative analyses measuring expressed behavior. The quest to understand the association between our latent unacknowledged desires and political behavior that characterized the first period was replaced by the study of political attitudes, beliefs, values, and vote choices. The dominant theoretical framework during this phase centered around social psychological models of decision-making and socialization. The publication of the *American Voter* by a group of political scientists at the University of Michigan is the most prominent research example of this era and one of the most influential studies of all time in social science (Campbell et al., 1960). Campbell and his colleagues drew on an extensive nationwide sample asking a plethora of questions about citizens' voting behavior. One

Sampling: The selection of a subgroup of a population to study and reach conclusions about the whole population.

Psychometric scales: Questionnaires, usually consisting of several questions, that are administered to a population to measure key psychological orientations.

Party identification: A long-term psychological attachment to a specific political party.

of the key concepts they described was **party identification**, which referred to a long-term psychological attachment to a specific political party. They discovered that this attachment was developed during adolescence through direct family transmission, particularly in families with high levels of political interest. Party identification remained stable and even strengthened across the life span, but at the same time did not necessarily correspond to an awareness about the ideological differences between the two main US political parties.

This second era focusing on behavior, falls more within the scope of political science rather than psychology as many of the leading scholars of the time were based in politics departments (Sullivan et al., 2002). However, there were several notable exceptions that were psychological in focus, originating mostly from the field of social psychology. These concerned **intra**- and **intergroup relationships** and dynamics. Regarding the former, the infamous Milgram experiment (Milgram, 1963) demonstrated that ordinary citizens were willing to administer lethal electric shocks in response to the psychological need to obey authority (see Chapter 5). The study had a profound impact on political psychology as it underscored the powerful role of context in human behavior, showing that under specific circumstances everyday people can be compelled to commit acts of evil regardless of their personalities. On the other hand, the foundational studies by Muzafer Sherif on the conditions under which intergroup conflict arises and resolves (Sherif, 1961, see also Chapter 6) remain very influential six decades after their publication and are particularly useful for understanding contemporary political phenomena such as the origins and expressions of increased partisan hostility and the justification of political violence (e.g., Kalmoe & Mason, 2022).

The third stage of political psychology research began around the 1970s and dominated the 1980s and part of the 1990s. This period is characterized by the shift toward **cognitive psychology** and especially research on memory and decision-making under conditions of limited information. The focus during this era was on political information processing in all of its forms. Research focused on how voters acquire, store in memory, and recall political information that they receive from their immediate environment or the mass media and how this information interacts with prior levels of political knowledge and ideological orientations to shape political decisions (e.g., Conover & Feldman, 1984; Fiske et al., 1983).

Cognitive psychology: A subfield of psychology dedicated to the study of information processing, memory, and problem solving.

The field of political psychology grew significantly in the 1990s, with a number of academic programs being introduced in the United States and Europe. These evolutions ushered in a fourth era of political psychological inquiry. On the one hand, research returned to older questions such as the role of personality in political behavior or information processing using novel theoretical and methodological tools (e.g., Sniderman et al., 1991; Zaller, 1992). On the other hand, post-1990 political psychology was characterized by the introduction of new theoretical concepts and research themes. These included innovative research on the role of emotions in political decision-making (Marcus & MacKuen, 1993). Further, there were significant advancements in our understanding of intergroup attitudes through the identification of new individual differences such as **social dominance orientation** (Pratto et al., 1994) which help us understand the psychological motivations behind prejudice and discrimination as well as the psychological underpinnings of political ideologies.

Social dominance orientation: A long-term psychological preference for maintaining social inequality and dominating over low-status social groups.

Political psychology in the past two decades has witnessed a diversification in geographical scope and a notable rise in interdisciplinary approaches. The need to understand the relationship between psychological structures and political choices outside of Western, Educated, Industrialized, Rich, and Democratic (W.E.I.R.D.) context that we discussed in Chapter 1 has resulted in a number of important research programs focusing on Latin America, Africa, Asia, and the Middle East (e.g., Hawi et al., 2022; Rivera Pichardo et al., 2022a; see also Chapter 11). These programs develop novel political psychological theories to explain political outcomes in specific national contexts (e.g., Mukashema & Mullet, 2015) test hypotheses that are considered universal within the discipline in new empirical settings (e.g., Owuamalam & Matos, 2019), or develop new theories intended to fapply across contexts (e.g,. Rivera Pichardo et al., 2022b). Research on emotional reactions toward authoritarian regimes (Montiel & Uyheng, 2020), pedagogical interventions to counter political misinformation (Badrinathan, 2021), psychological interventions to reduce prejudice toward refugees (Larson & Lewis, 2025), or personality and support for autocratic forms of governance (Armendáriz Miranda, 2022) provide only some examples of internationally leading political psychology research taking place outside of W.E.I.R.D contexts.

Further, political psychology is now increasingly becoming interdisciplinary drawing in particular on insights from **evolutionary biology**, **genetics**, and **neuroscience** (e.g., Hatemi & McDermott, 2011). The seemingly unlikely marriage between political psychology and biology brings a wealth of theoretical and methodological tools to better understand human motivation in

Evolutionary biology: A subfield of biology investigating the evolution of life.

Genetics: A branch of biology studying genes, inherited traits, and variation in organisms.

Neuroscience: A scientific discipline studying the nervous system with a focus on the structure and function of the brain.

Neuroimaging: A scientific discipline that studies brain anatomy and function through imaging techniques.

politics. For instance, a large stream of research identifies a genetic component in the transmission of political preferences above and beyond parental influence or the social environment (Funk et al., 2013). This finding challenges the view that our political preferences are entirely shaped by societal factors. It underlies instead that we are born with an innate disposition to find some broad political concepts (e.g., attitudes toward equality or severity of punishment) more appealing than others (Hatemi & McDermott, 2011). These findings have considerable implications for our understanding of ideology as they point to the conclusion that all people are ideological even if they sometimes lack the political information to express these preferences. Further, they underscore the limits of persuasion and deliberation. Another stream of contemporary political psychology research draws on theoretical and methodological insights from neuroscience to understand how the brain processes political stimuli (see Zmigrod & Tsakiris, 2021 for an overview). Drawing on methods such as **neuroimaging**, researchers can observe which parts of the brain become activated when exposed to political content (e.g., Moore et al., 2021), or whether liberals and conservatives display neurocognitive differences in information processing or sensitivity to threats (e.g., Amodio et al., 2007; Bakker et al., 2020).

Conclusion

This chapter provided a historical overview of political psychological thought and a presentation of the five eras of modern political psychology research. For many classical philosophers, the study of politics is the study of human nature, the study of our passions, virtues, and limitations. In this respect, it is impossible to disentangle the political – our collective organization and distribution of resources – from the psychological – our individual qualities. Political psychology research in the last eight decades has offered fascinating insights into the ways in which our psychological structures shape our political choices and decision-making processes, advancing the understanding of both our human nature and our political organization. As I discuss in the remaining chapters of this book, contemporary political psychology provides important interpretive theoretical tools for understanding modern societal challenges such as the rise of authoritarianism across different parts of the globe, the persistence of discrimination, our attachment to social identities, or the backlash against civil liberties. As Jost and Sidanius put it two decades ago: "To know everything there is to know about the world of politics in theory and in practice, one must be, among other things, an expert in psychology" (2004, p. 1). This cannot be more pertinent today.

Further Reading

Marcus, G. E. (2013). *Political psychology: Neuroscience, genetics, and politics*. Oxford: Oxford University Press.
Sears, D. O., Huddy, L., & Jervis, R. (2003). The psychologies underlying political psychology. In D. O. Sears, L. Huddy, & R. Jervis (Eds.), *The Oxford handbook of political psychology* (pp. 3–19). Oxford: Oxford University Press.

References

Adorno, T. W., Frenkel-Brunswik, E., Levinson, D. J., & Sanford, R. N. (1950). *The authoritarian personality*. New York: Harper and Row.
Amodio, D. M., Jost, J. T., Master, S. L., & Yee, C. M. (2007). Neurocognitive correlates of liberalism and conservatism. *Nature Neuroscience*, *10* (10), 1246–1247.
Aristotle. (1998). *Politics*. Oxford: Oxford University Press.
Armendáriz Miranda, P. (2022). Explaining autocratic support: The varying effects of threat on personality. *Political Psychology*, *43* (6), 993–1007.
Badrinathan, S. (2021). Educative interventions to combat misinformation: Evidence from a field experiment in India. *American Political Science Review*, *115* (4), 1325–1341.
Bakker, B. N., Schumacher, G., Gothreau, C., & Arceneaux, K. (2020). Conservatives and liberals have similar physiological responses to threats. *Nature Human Behaviour*, *4* (6), 613–621.
Campbell, A., Converse, P. E., Miller, W. E., & Stokes, D. E. (1960) *The American voter*. New York: Wiley.
Conover, P. J., & Feldman, S. (1984). How people organize the political world: A schematic model. *American Journal of Political Science*, *28* (1), 95–126.
Fiske, S. T., Kinder, D. R., & Larter, W. M. (1983). The novice and the expert: Knowledge-based strategies in political cognition. *Journal of Experimental Social Psychology*, *19* (4), 381–400.
Funk, C. L., Smith, K. B., Alford, J. R., Hibbing, M. V., Eaton, N. R., Krueger, R. F., Eaves, L. J., & Hibbing, J. R. (2013). Genetic and environmental transmission of political orientations. *Political Psychology*, *34* (6), 805–819.
Hatemi, P. K., & McDermott, R. (Eds.). (2011). *Man is by nature a political animal: Evolution, biology, and politics*. Chicago: University of Chicago Press.
Hawi, D., Bou Zeineddine, F., Saab, R., Ayanian, A. H., & Harb, C. (2022). Political psychology in the Arab region: A commentary on navigating research in unstable contexts. In D. Osborne & C. G. Sibley (Eds.), *The Cambridge handbook of political psychology* (pp. 624–639). Cambridge: Cambridge University Press.

Hobbes, T. (1996). Leviathan (R. Tuck, Ed.). Cambridge: Cambridge University Press. (Original work published 1651).
Hobbes, T. (1998). *On the citizen*. Cambridge: Cambridge University Press. (Original work published 1642).
Jost, J. T., & Sidanius, J. (Eds.). (2004). *Political psychology: Key readings*. New York: Psychology Press.
Jost, J. T., Stern, C., Rule, N. O., & Sterling, J. (2017). The politics of fear: Is there an ideological asymmetry in existential motivation?. *Social Cognition*, *35*(4), 324–353.
Kalmoe, N. P., & Mason, L. (2022). Radical American partisanship: Mapping violent hostility, its causes, and the consequences for democracy. In *Radical American partisanship*. Chicago: University of Chicago Press.
Larson, J. M., & Lewis, J. I. (2025). Reducing prejudice toward refugees: Evidence that social networks influence attitude change in Uganda. *American Political Science Review*, *119*(1), 349–367.
Lasswell, H. D. (2016). *Psychopathology and politics*. Chicago, IL: University of Chicago Press. (Original work published 1930).
Le Bon, G. (1960). *The crowd: A study of the popular mind*. New York, NY: Viking. (Original work published 1895).
Machiavelli, N. (2021). *The prince*. Asturias: King Solomon. (Original work published 1532).
Marcus, G. E. (2001). Political psychology: A personal view. In K. R. Monroe (Ed.), *Political psychology* (pp. 103–114). New York: Psychology Press.
Marcus, G. E., & MacKuen, M. B. (1993). Anxiety, enthusiasm, and the vote: The emotional underpinnings of learning and involvement during presidential campaigns. *American Political Science Review*, *87*(3), 672–685.
Marcus, G. E., Neuman, W. R., & MacKuen, M. (2000). *Affective intelligence and political judgment*. Chicago: University of Chicago Press.
McGuire, W. J. (1993). The Poly-Psy relationship: Three phases of a long affair. In S. Iyengar & W. J. McGuire (Eds.), *Explorations in political psychology* (pp. 9–35). Durham: Duke University Press.
Milgram, S. (1963). Behavioral study of obedience. *The Journal of Abnormal and Social Psychology*, *67*(4), 371.
Montiel, C. J., & Uyheng, J. (2020). Mapping contentious collective emotions in a populist democracy: Duterte's push for Philippine federalism. *Political Psychology*, *41*(4), 737–754.
Moore, A., Hong, S., & Cram, L. (2021). Trust in information, political identity and the brain: An interdisciplinary fMRI study. *Philosophical Transactions of the Royal Society B*, *376*(1822), 20200140.
Mukashema, I., & Mullet, E. (2015). Attribution of guilt to offspring of perpetrators of the genocide: Rwandan people's perspectives. *Conflict Resolution Quarterly*, *33*(1), 75–98.
Neblo, M. A. (2007). Philosophical psychology with political intent. In W. R. Neuman, G. E. Marcus, A. N. Crigler, & M. MacKuen (Eds.), *The affect effect: Dynamics of emotion in political thinking and behavior* (pp. 25–47). Chicago: University of Chicago Press.
Owuamalam, C. K., & Matos, A. S. (2019). Do egalitarians always help the disadvantaged more than the advantaged? Testing a value-norm conflict hypothesis in Malaysia. *Asian Journal of Social Psychology*, *22*(2), 151–162.
Plato. (2012). *Republic*. London: Penguin.

Rivera Pichardo, E. J., Jost, J. T., & Benet-Martínez, V. (2022a). Internalization of inferiority and colonial system justification: The case of Puerto Rico. *Journal of Social Issues*, *78* (1), 79–106.
Rivera Pichardo, E. J., Vargas Salfate, S., & Jost, J. T. (2022b). Political psychology in the global South. In D. Osborne & C. G. Sibley (Eds.), *The Cambridge handbook of political psychology*. Cambridge: Cambridge University Press.
Pratto, F., Sidanius, J., Stallworth, L. M., & Malle, B. F. (1994). Social dominance orientation: A personality variable predicting social and political attitudes. *Journal of Personality and Social Psychology*, *67* (4), 741.
Sherif, M. (1961). *Intergroup conflict and cooperation: The Robbers Cave experiment*. Norman: University of Oklahoma Institute of Group Relations.
Sniderman, P. M., Brody, R. A., & Tetlock, P. E. (1991). *Reasoning and choice: Explorations in political psychology*. Cambridge: Cambridge University Press.
Sullivan, J. L., Rahn, W. M., & Rudolph, T. (2002). The contours of political psychology: Situating research on political information processing. In J. H. Kuklinski (Ed.), *Thinking about political psychology* (pp. 23–47). Cambridge: Cambridge University Press.
Wallas, G. (1908). *Human nature in politics*. New York: AA Knopf.
Zaller, J. (1992). *The nature and origins of mass opinion*. Cambridge: Cambridge University Press.
Zmigrod, L., & Tsakiris, M. (2021). Computational and neurocognitive approaches to the political brain: Key insights and future avenues for political neuroscience. *Philosophical Transactions of the Royal Society B*, *376* (1822), 20200130.

Section 2

Key Theories

Chapter 3

Authoritarianism

Introduction

Early psychological studies of the followers of authoritarian leaders began in the 1940s in the shadow of the rise of the Nazi party in Germany and intensified after the full extent of the atrocities – and particularly the Holocaust – was revealed. The questions that motivated this work were of fundamental importance for post-Second World War societies: How can citizens willingly submit their liberty to fascist leaders? And how can they exhibit such propensity for cruelty and evil against minorities, outgroups, and political opponents? These questions became particularly pressing during the late 1940s and early 1950s. This was the period of systematic, unfounded persecutions against government agents, intellectuals, and public figures in the United States, that came to be known as McCarthyism. It was also the period when the Apartheid laws were installed in South Africa, legalizing and systematizing prejudice and racial segregation. These events intensified the fear that a Nazi-type regime could be reinstated in other democracies, and the reasons why ordinary citizens could turn to fervent authoritarian supporters cried for explanation.

The starting point of work exploring the authoritarian psyche was to dismiss popular explanations of public support for authoritarian movements. These explained the phenomenon on the basis of oppression or deception of the people in authoritarian regimes by authoritarian leaders (Fromm, 1941). Instead, the answer to the question of mass authoritarian support was sought in the *character* of the authoritarian follower that inclined them to freely and willingly follow these types of leaders. The psychological factor in this early line of work was not in isolation with the contemporary social and economic environment but rather emerged as a product of it (Adorno et al., 1950; Fromm, 1994). Erich Fromm, a pioneer sociologist and psychologist, who was one of the earliest scholars of the psychology of **authoritarianism**, argued that

Authoritarianism: A long-term individual disposition to support authoritarian leaders.

DOI: 10.4324/9781003460084-5

the authoritarian character develops as a response to the anxiety and isolation brought about by the growing freedom and individualization of the industrial society (1994).

More than eight decades have passed since the first conceptualization of authoritarianism as a psychological characteristic and the concept remains alarmingly relevant today. Despite the establishment of international institutions aimed at safeguarding democracy, economic growth, and the expansion of tertiary education, many societies are experiencing a resurgence of authoritarianism as a response to immigration and increased demands for minority rights. The electoral success of authoritarian populist leaders like Trump in the United States, Bolsonaro in Brazil, Le Pen in France, Orban in Hungary, or Duterte in the Philippines and the accommodation of extreme right demands in the platforms of mainstream conservative parties (Brown et al., 2023), pose existential dangers to liberal democracy. Understanding the appeal of authoritarian leaders has been one of the primary goals of political psychology. This goal contributed much to political psychology's birth as a subfield within the social sciences and is still a central aspect of its contemporary importance. This chapter engages with the nature and dynamics of the psychological adaptation of authoritarianism.

The Authoritarian Personality

The first systematic effort to analyze authoritarianism as an enduring psychological trait was *The Authoritarian Personality* (Adorno et al., 1950), a voluminous book written during and shortly after the Second World War. It was the result of a collaboration between the prominent social theorist Theodor Adorno and Else Frenkel-Brunswik, Daniel Levinson, and Nevitt Sanford, a group of psychologists based at the University of Berkeley in California. The aim of this book was to assess the fascist inclinations in the United States by focusing on the "potentially fascistic individual, one whose structure is such to render him particularly susceptible to anti-democratic propaganda" (1950, p. 1).

The authors drew heavily on Freudian psychology to argue that political attitudes and beliefs stem from deep psychological processes. They described authoritarianism as a personality type that found its roots in childhood. Specifically, they located the development of authoritarianism in the manner in which children are socialized and trained in households consisting of a stern and distant paternal figure and a submissive mother. Growing up in this type of household was marked by exaggerated discipline and control that did not allow any space for pleasure or the fulfillment of fundamental psychological needs. The main idea behind the development of authoritarianism was that a child growing up in such an environment was likely to develop intense hostility toward the exaggerated parental discipline that could then be easily displaced and turn into aggression and hatred toward minorities and social deviants. The authoritarian personality consisted of nine distinct but interrelated traits that formed a common personality type that was characterized by *anti-Semitism*, *prejudice and ethnocentrism*, *fascistic tendencies*, and *political and economic conservatism*. The nine traits together with their original definitions are presented in Table 3.1.

Many of these traits, such as anti-intellectualism, cynicism, and an emphasis on toughness and strength are seemingly unrelated to politics. However, they remain visible among far-right followers across the world, eight decades after they were first described. But how did the authors come up with these specific nine traits? The first step was the administration of questionnaires measuring anti-Semitism, ethnocentrism, and conservatism to a sample of White American adults, largely collected from various social clubs. Through these questionnaires the authors identified citizens who scored high in prejudice, ethnocentrism, and anti-democratic tendencies. Consequently, they chose some of the people scoring very high and some of the people scoring very low on the scales and undertook clinical sessions with them. By contrasting the experiences of high and low scorers they were able to uncover common themes and behavioral patterns among the most prejudiced. They focused on personal histories, family

Table 3.1 The Nine Components of the Authoritarian Personality (Adorno et al., 1950, Chapter 7)

Trait	*Description*
Conventionalism and adherence to middle-class values	"Rigid adherence to middle-class values"
Authoritarian submission	"Submissive, uncritical attitude toward idealized moral authorities of the ingroup"
Authoritarian aggression	"Tendency to be on the lookout for, and to condemn, reject and punish people who violate conventional norms"
Anti-intraception	"Opposition to the subjective, the imaginative, the tender-minded"
Superstition and stereotypy	"The belief in mystical determinants of the individual's fate; the disposition to think in rigid categories"
Power and toughness	"Preoccupation with the dominance-submission strong-weak, leader-follower dimension; identification with power figures; exaggerated assertion of strength and toughness"
Destructiveness and cynicism	"Generalized hostility, vilification of the human"
Sex	"Exaggerated concern with sexual going-ons"
Projectivity	"The disposition to believe that wild and dangerous things go on in the world; the projection outwards of unconscious emotional impulses"

environment, personal relationships, as well as fears and desires. The nine traits reflected the motifs that were revealed in the clinical sessions and differentiated those scoring high in prejudice from the low scorers.

The third step was to construct a scale that was based on these motifs. The authors called it the **F-scale**, F standing for fascism. The F-scale could be used to measure the authoritarian tendencies of mass publics in mass quantitative surveys, providing insights on the fascistic potential of the United States. This scale asked respondents the extent to which they agreed or disagree with statements that captured the nine traits (e.g., "Homosexuality is a particularly rotten form of delinquency and ought to be severely punished" for *authoritarian aggression*, "too many people today are living in an unnatural, soft way; we should return to the fundamentals, to a more red-blooded active way of life" for *power and toughness* or "If people would talk less and work more, everybody would be better off" for *anti-intraception*). Despite being seemingly unrelated to the phenomenon it sought to explain the F-scale correlated with anti-Semitism, ethnocentrism, and conservatism. In other words, it could predict prejudice and anti-democratic potential by asking about a person's deeper psychological traits and inclinations, hence providing a valuable tool for understanding the psychology of authoritarian followers.

F-scale: Developed by the authors of the Authoritarian Personality, the F-scale was a psychological measure consisting of several questions aiming at measuring a respondent's proclivity toward fascism.

Despite its profound influence in the field of political psychology, *The Authoritarian Personality* received widespread criticism both on its theoretical foundations and its methodology (e.g., Stone, 1980). Contemporary social and political psychologists questioned the theory on the basis of its strong dependence on the Freudian psychoanalytic framework that was increasingly criticized in psychological research (Altemeyer, 1981). Others questioned the coherence of the traits. For example, superstition and stereotypy are taxonomized as a common trait despite not really referring to the same thing (Altemeyer, 1981). Another point of criticism concerned flaws in the methodology. Samples used to validate the F-scale, for example, included prison inmates who were hardly an ideal sample for generalizing the findings. Moreover, the wording of the F-scale items was non-balanced, that is, one could achieve the highest authoritarianism score by simply agreeing with the statements that were presented, which was a serious flaw of the questionnaire (Brown, 1965). Critically, more sophisticated statistical analyses showed that the nine traits of the Authoritarian Personality had low correlations between them and hence did not seem to form a coherent personality type (Altemeyer, 1981; Brown, 1965).

The Revival of the Study of Authoritarianism – Right-Wing Authoritarianism

Despite the criticism on the theoretical and empirical foundations of the *Authoritarian Personality*, the idea that prejudice and anti-democratic tendencies stem from deeper psychological structures persisted among social and political psychologists. Bob Altemeyer offered a major reconceptualization of authoritarianism that attempted to overcome the weaknesses of the *Authoritarian Personality* (1981, 1988, 1996). His conceptualization of authoritarianism, termed **Right-Wing Authoritarianism (RWA)**, did not refer to a personality trait but instead to a cluster of attitudes that is rooted in personality but is also affected by aspects of one's social environment.

Right-wing authoritarianism: A refinement of the original concept of authoritarianism in the 1980s, sees authoritarianism as a cluster of attitudes that include conventionalism, authoritarian submission, and authoritarian aggression.

Altemeyer simplified the theory to a significant extent. He rejected the complex psychoanalytic framework used by the authors of the *Authoritarian Personality* (1981). Instead, he argued that authoritarian tendencies are *learned* by the family and the broader social environment rather than constituting an expression of depressed hostility toward one's parents. The process he described was fairly simple: children tend to observe their parents and imitate their behavior. Moreover, they learn directly from their parents which actions and attitudes are acceptable and which are not, being rewarded for correct behavior and punished for incorrect behavior. The circle of early life influencers also extends to grandfathers, older siblings, teachers, or even people with no direct contact with the child, such as media figures. Even though Altemeyer considered childhood and adolescence critical in the development of authoritarianism, he saw authoritarianism as a dynamic and adjustable process, influenced by the social environment. The circle of influence in adulthood can include friends, work colleagues, or neighbors, who may reinforce or weaken authoritarian tendencies. For example, if an authoritarian adolescent attends university, their orientation may change through the exposure to new sets of norms and new standards of what constitutes acceptable behavior and acceptable attitudes. Hence, according to Altemeyer, "neither the organization nor the level of authoritarianism is ever set in concrete" (1981, p. 258).

The second major refinement concerned the authoritarian traits themselves. Altemeyer retained only three of the original nine components of the Authoritarian Personality: *Conventionalism*, which refers to "a high degree of adherence to the social conventions which are perceived to be endorsed by society and its established authorities"; *Authoritarian Submission* – "a high degree of submission to the authorities who are perceived to be established and legitimate in the society in which one lives"; and *Authoritarian Aggression*, which refers to "a general aggressiveness, directed against various persons, which is perceived to be sanctioned by established authorities" (Altemeyer, 1981, p. 148).

According to Altemeyer Right-Wing authoritarians have strong submissive and aggressive impulses. They bow down to established authorities and the norms they advocate, even if they do not abide by them in their daily lives. On the other hand, they have strong aggressive and punitive inclinations expressed either as a desire to harm or, more often, as support for cruelty toward people who lead unconventional lifestyles or are systematically targeted by the established authorities, such as religious and sexual minorities, immigrants, drug users, or the homeless. For example, support for police violence runs high among right-wing authoritarians, as it involves the abuse of individuals who are targeted by established authorities (Altemeyer, 1981, pp. 152–153). Moreover, authoritarians tend to see the world as a threatening place on the brink of moral collapse by those who do not cherish conventional norms (Altemeyer, 1981, 1998). At the same time, they are self-righteous as they consider themselves the protectors of morality, a characteristic that allows them to punish social deviants. Finally, they tend to interact with like-minded people which often leads them to mistakenly perceive themselves as part of a "silent majority" that is oppressed by their political enemies (Altemeyer, 1998, pp. 86–87).

Altemeyer developed the RWA scale as an alternative to the F-scale. The original scale included 30 items to capture each of the three dimensions. It asked people the extent to which they agreed or disagreed with statements such as: "What our country really needs is a strong, determined leader who will crush evil, and take us back to our true path"; "It would be best for everyone if the proper authorities censored magazines so that people would not get their hands on trashy and disgusting material"; "The facts on crime, sexual immorality, and the recent public disorders all show we have to crack down harder on deviant groups and troublemakers if we are going to save our moral standards and preserve law and order".

Altemeyer's work renewed the interest in the psychological trait of authoritarianism, spurring a large and productive wave of research up until this day. There have been many studies showing a strong correlation between RWA and diverse expressions of prejudice, conservatism, and support for far-right parties and leaders in different countries (e.g., Altemeyer, 1998; Choma & Hanoch, 2017; Peresman et al., 2021). However, as was the case with the *Authoritarian Personality,* RWA has also been the focus of criticism both in terms of conceptualization and measurement. One line of criticism argues that the theory falls short of explaining how conventionalism, aggression, and submission are connected in a psychological sense (Engelhardt et al., 2023). Other critics have argued that the RWA scale is partly tautological in the sense that it directly measures the social and political attitudes that it is designed to predict (e.g., Engelhardt et al., 2023; Feldman, 2003). In other words, instead of capturing a psychological motivation of prejudice, the RWA rather captures the *outcomes* of prejudice by directly asking respondents about their attitudes toward minorities and social deviants (Feldman, 2003). Others notice that the items in the scale are worded in a way that resembles the discourse style of authoritarian leaders, which poses a problem as respondents may agree with the items because it resembles the language of their preferred political leaders (Engelhardt et al., 2023).

Authoritarianism as Social Conformity

Considering these criticisms, Stanley Feldman and his colleagues proposed a second major theoretical and empirical refinement of the psychological disposition of authoritarianism (Engelhardt et al., 2023; Feldman, 2003, 2020; see also Stenner, 2005). Their conceptualization centers around the trade-off between personal autonomy and social control, an inescapable aspect of living in any society. Individuals value autonomy and independence but at the same time being a member of a human society requires at least some conformity with social norms. Hence, autonomy and social control may sometimes represent antagonistic values. This trade-off can be represented as a scale. On one end of the scale, there exists a desire for personal autonomy, independence, and individual expression. People who would place themselves there are more committed to freedom of expression, supportive of civil liberties, and against state control in individuals' lives. Further, they are more likely to react favorably to those with a lifestyle that does not conform to the social mainstream. On the one end of this scale there exists a desire for social homogeneity that fosters the development of collective social norms. This is the authoritarian end. People who place themselves there are motivated to maintain social cohesion. Thus, they exhibit rejection or punitive attitudes toward people who deviate from dominant social norms and live unconventional lifestyles, such as immigrants, ethnic minorities, or LGBTQI+ members. Hence, according to Feldman and his colleagues, the psychological motivation behind prejudice and the endorsement of authoritarian leaders is the desire to strengthen social homogeneity. As Stenner summarizes: "authoritarianism is an individual predisposition concerned with the appropriate balance between group authority and uniformity on the one hand, and individual autonomy and diversity, on the other" (2005, p. 14). Importantly, this definition leaves out authoritarian aggression and submission that constitute the core of the authoritarian disposition in earlier works, considering them as consequences of the desire for social control rather than constitutive elements of authoritarianism (see Feldman & Weber, 2023).

Feldman and colleagues proposed a new scale to measure authoritarianism, which aims at capturing the social control versus personal autonomy trade-off.

They chose to focus on child-rearing ideals (Engelhardt et al., 2023; Feldman, 2003). The reason is that child socialization touches on profound human values across societies and is informative of one's general life ideals and objectives (Feldman & Stenner, 1997). Another reason is that the items have no apparent political content and thus allow for the measurement of authoritarianism without the tautology issues that characterized the RWA scale. Finally, they offer the additional advantage of comparability across time and space as they touch deeper held value inclinations rather than attitudes toward policies or groups which are subject to change (as was the case with RWA).

The questions ask respondents to choose over different child-rearing values, usually asked as follows:

Although there are a number of qualities that people feel children should have, every person thinks that some are more important than others. I am going to read you pairs of desirable qualities. Please tell me which one you think is more important for a child to have:

1 *Independence versus respect for elders*
2 *Obedience versus self-reliance*
3 *Curiosity versus good manners*
4 *Being considerate versus being well-behaved*

The responses "respectful of their elders", "obedient", "well behaved", and "good mannered" denote the authoritarian response. Of course, most parents would like their children to have both sets of qualities that each question presents. Forcing a choice however can reveal a lot about whether they prioritize social control over personal autonomy or in other words their levels of authoritarianism. The child-rearing scale has been found to predict diverse manifestations of authoritarianism in the United States, Europe, and Latin America. These include prejudice and ethnic intolerance, support for restricting civil liberties, as well as voting for far-right parties and candidates (Bakker et al., 2021; Helminen et al., 2024; Vasilopoulos & Lachat, 2018).

Despite its increasing popularity in political psychology research, the child-rearing scale has received criticism. For instance, Napier and Jost (2008) argue that reducing authoritarianism to preferences for conventionalism and obedience over personal autonomy neglects important dimensions that characterize authoritarian followers, such as aggression, cognitive rigidity, or cynicism which need to be studied as fundamental elements of authoritarianism and not mere consequences. Pérez and Hetherington raised doubt about the cross-racial validity of the scale in the US context, showing that the interpretation of the questions is not the same for Whites and African Americans (2014).

Authoritarianism and Threat

Most approaches of authoritarianism describe a long-term individual orientation that is relatively resistant to change. At the same time endorsing authoritarian solutions can also be a momentary response to a significant external threat. There is an abundance of evidence that support for authoritarian policies or leaders increases in the light of threats such as wars, terror attacks, economic shocks, or pandemics (e.g., Davis & Silver, 2004; Hetherington & Suhay, 2011; Vasilopoulos et al., 2023). The association between threat and different manifestations of authoritarianism, such as aggression toward outgroups or punitiveness has been noted for several decades. Sales (1973) and Doty et al. (1991) investigated the extent to which objective behavioral measures of authoritarianism increased in the United States during high-threat periods (characterized by economic stagnation, increased likelihood of war, and increased crime), compared to low-threat periods. Drawing on archival research, they found an increase in a surprisingly diverse set of behavioral manifestations of authoritarianism that directly corresponded to the nine components of Adorno et al.'s authoritarian syndrome. Their measures included the number of anti-Semitic incidents, number of boxing matches, purchases of dogs from powerful breeds, beliefs in astrology, production of violent pornographic movies, as well as measures of prejudice.

Despite the consensus on the association between threat and authoritarianism, there exists scholarly disagreement on who is more prone to endorsing authoritarian policies and candidates in the light of threat. Some contend that threat does not change the levels of authoritarianism but rather activates it. This means that those who already have an authoritarian disposition will become even more prejudiced, aggressive, and willing to endorse authoritarian policies in the light of threat (e.g., Feldman, 2003; Feldman & Stenner, 1997). An example here would be a person who may hold authoritarian beliefs but does not act on them unless they feel some kind of personal or societal threat, such as an economic recession. An alternative perspective argues that threat makes individuals without an authoritarian disposition resemble those with a long-term authoritarian inclination (Hetherington & Suhay, 2011). The argument here is that threat makes non-authoritarians endorse authoritarian preferences that they would normally disagree with. Finally, a third stream of studies finds that both tendencies occur simultaneously depending on appraisals of the threat (Vasilopoulos et al, 2018).

Left-Wing Authoritarianism

Almost immediately after the publication of the *Authoritarian Personality* some researchers suggested that "at the left pole of their continuum, there is to be found an authoritarian impressively like the Authoritarianism of the Right" (Shils, 1954, p. 38). This argument has been a point of contention among political psychologists for decades and still continues to generate intense scholarly debate. By and large it rests on two grounds. First, proponents of the **Left-Wing Authoritarianism** (LWA) thesis draw parallelism between the communist and fascist regimes of the 20th century in terms of submission to authority, rigidity, and aggression toward political opponents all of which constitute, as we saw above, fundamental aspects of authoritarianism (Shils, 1954). Second, this argument also highlights presumed resemblances between the psychological motivations of far-left and far-right supporters. For instance, Eysenck (2018) argues that authoritarianism should run high among both extremes of the ideological spectrum as both far-left and far-right supporters tend to be rigid, inflexible, and tough-minded. On the other hand, he argued that those with more moderate views are more humanistic, accepting, and compassionate.

Left-wing authoritarianism: The hypothesis that individuals with personality characteristics similar to Right-Wing authoritarians can also be found on the left end of the ideological spectrum.

There is indeed evidence that authoritarianism in former communist states is associated with support for the socialist ideology and for communist parties. For instance, in a series of studies in Russia in the 1980s and early 1990s, McFarland found that people scoring high on an adjusted version of the RWA scale were anti-capitalist and strongly endorsing egalitarianism, which represented the conventional value system in a Communist society (McFarland et al., 1996). At the same time, it has been much harder to find large numbers of left-wing authoritarians in Western societies, where authoritarianism has time and again been found to correlate with conservatism (Nilsson & Jost, 2020). As Altemeyer (1981, p. 151) puts it, "The radical leftists of the late 1960s [in the USA] who were dynamiting buildings … may be called doctrinaire, dogmatic, fanatic, and many other things. But they were not submissive to established authorities, nor were they particularly conventional".

Based on the lack of empirical evidence on large numbers of left-wing authoritarians in the non-communist world, LWA has been named "the Loch Ness monster of political psychology" (Altemeyer, 1996). The problem is that very few people score high in these types of scales to be considered as evidence of a mass authoritarian tendency of the political Left that is equal to or similar with what is found on the Right (e.g., Altemeyer, 1996; Van Hiel et al., 2006). Conway and colleagues (2018) created a LWA scale, similar to the one used to measure RWA, for capturing the trait. Critics, however, point to serious content inconsistencies between the LWA and RWA scales (e.g., Nilsson, 2024). For instance, where the RWA scale asks respondents to agree or disagree with the statement "Gays and lesbians are just as healthy and moral as anybody else" (with disagreement indicating the authoritarian response), the LWA scale asks whether respondents agree or disagree with the statement that "Christian fundamentalists are just as healthy and moral as anybody else".

Social Dominance Orientation – The "Other" Authoritarian Personality

In the mid-1990s Felicia Pratto, Jim Sidanius, and their colleagues introduced a general attitudinal orientation called **Social Dominance Orientation** (**SDO** – Pratto et al., 1994). While similar to authoritarianism in terms of its correlation with prejudice, it was different in its conceptualization to the extent that it is now accepted as a second, independent dimension. SDO captures whether one prefers intergroup relations to be equal as opposed to hierarchical and "the extent to which one desires that one's in-group dominate and be superior to outgroups" (Pratto et al., 1994, p. 742; see also Sidanius et al., 2004). SDO is strongly associated with prejudice but through a different psychological pathway than authoritarianism. People scoring high in SDO see the world as consisting of superior and inferior social groups. They endorse intergroup dominance and are opposed to social equality, supporting policies that maintain social inequality or lead to the oppression of low-status groups. They are driven by a "ruthless, amoral struggle for resources and power in which might is right and winning is everything" (Duckitt et al., 2002, p. 92). Whereas authoritarians tend to be conformist and driven toward tradition and structure, social dominators tend to be hedonistic and power-driven. On the other end, those scoring low in SDO are characterized by egalitarian beliefs and altruistic feelings (Duckitt et al., 2002).

> **Social Dominance Orientation:** A psychological orientation combining preference for hierarchical intergroup relations with a desire to dominate over outgroups.

Even though authoritarianism (measured in most cases with the RWA scale) and SDO generally correlate, both traits are predictive of conservatism and hostility toward a plethora of low-status social groups. SDO partly captures traits of authoritarianism that were present in the *Authoritarian Personality* study such as power and toughness or cynicism but were left out in the more recent refinements of the concept, which focus on conventionalism, submission, and aggression. Similarly to authoritarianism, SDO has been found to be associated with support for anti-immigration policies, generalized prejudice, and voting for far-right parties (Aichholzer & Zandonella, 2016). SDO is further associated with policies that maintain social and economic inequalities, such as opposition to welfare state policies and affirmative action, or the endorsement of hawkish foreign policies (Jedinger & Kaminski, 2024). At the same time there are some key differences between social dominators and authoritarians. Conventionalism and submission to established authorities, two central traits in authoritarianism, do not characterize social dominators (Altemeyer, 1998). Prejudice in authoritarianism "stems from an uncritical acceptance of statements made by respected authority figures that denigrate out-groups", while prejudice among social dominators is more "sophisticated, in the sense that it is more thought out because it stems from a need to justify the maintenance of societal status inequalities from which one benefits" (Duriez & Van Hiel, 2002, p. 1210). Another difference is that social dominators do not necessarily have a high sensitivity of threat: they do not see the world as a threatening place, but as a competitive, dog-eat-dog environment where one needs to be ruthless and dominant in order to thrive (Duriez & Van Hiel, 2002).

These differences are reflected in the sociodemographic antecedents of each orientation. Authoritarians, for instance, tend to be religious, while those scoring high in social dominance are not (Altemeyer, 1998). Unlike authoritarians, social dominators tend to be overwhelmingly male and predominantly young. Further, while education is strongly and negatively associated with authoritarianism, it is generally unassociated with SDO (Duriez & Van Hiel, 2002).

Conclusion

This chapter discussed some of the literature on the psychological trait of authoritarianism that aims to uncover the psychological substrates of prejudice and preferences for authoritarian leaders. The concept of authoritarianism has gone a long way since the publication of the *Authoritarian Personality* in 1950. As we underlined in this chapter there is a very vivid debate on the nature, measurement, and implications of the authoritarian syndrome. Altemeyer conceived authoritarianism as a cluster of attitudes encompassing aggression, submission, and conventionalism. Feldman sees authoritarianism as a consistent orientation toward social homogeneity and control to the expense of individual freedom and independence.

Despite the valuable insights we now have in the psychological motivations of authoritarian followers, some open questions remain. For instance, there is still scholarly disagreement on whether authoritarianism refers to a personality type, an "attitudinal cluster", or a "value orientation". This discussion is not about the choice of words but rather touches on the development of authoritarianism and the causal chain that connects it with prejudice. Some recent studies have questioned the extent to which authoritarianism (among other psychological traits) is truly an antecedent of prejudice and support for authoritarian candidates or a *consequence* of following authoritarian leaders (Bakker et al., 2021; Luttig, 2021; Vasilopoulos & Robinson, 2025). These authors argue that causality may run the other way, as politically like-minded people tend to interact more frequently with each other which leads to common norms and behavioral patterns. This in turn could be reflected in measures of general psychological characteristics such as authoritarianism (Bakker et al., 2021). Further, many people are aware of the stereotype that surrounds their political ingroup and hence may be responding accordingly when asked about their authoritarian attitudes (Bakker et al., 2021). In summary, these studies argue that far-right support drives authoritarianism rather than the other way around and that authoritarianism may not be only a cause of anti-immigration attitudes and far-right support but also a product of it. This has deeper implications for liberal democracy, as it suggests that anti-immigration attitudes may function as a gateway for the development of a broader authoritarian orientation among the electorate, and that when anti-immigration sentiment runs high a broader authoritarian turn could follow (Vasilopoulos & Robinson, 2025).

Further Readings

Feldman, S., & Weber, C. (2023). Authoritarianism and political conflict. In L. Huddy, D. O. Sears, J. S. Levy, & J. Jerit (Eds.), *The Oxford handbook of political psychology* (pp. 733–768). Oxford: Oxford University Press. A comprehensive summary of authoritarianism research.

Hetherington, M., & Weiler, J. (2018). *Prius or pickup?: How the answers to four simple questions explain America's great divide.* Boston, MA: Houghton Mifflin. A fascinating overview of research in authoritarianism and its relevance for understanding contemporary political divisions.

https://feministvoices.com/profiles/else-frenkel-brunswik: A short biography of Else Frenkel-Brunswik, one of the authors of the Authoritarian Personality.

https://theauthoritarians.org/: Here you can download a free copy of *The Authoritarians,* an accessible summary of the research of Bob Altemeyer, as well other works on authoritarianism by the same author.

References

Adorno, T. W., Frenkel-Brunswik, E., Levinson, D. J., & Nevitt Sanford, R. (1950). *The authoritarian personality.* New York: Harper & Row.

Aichholzer, J., & Zandonella, M. (2016). Psychological bases of support for radical right parties. *Personality and Individual Differences, 96,* 185–190.

Altemeyer, B. (1981). *Right-wing authoritarianism.* Manitoba: University of Manitoba Press.

Altemeyer, B. (1988). *Enemies of freedom: Understanding right-wing authoritarianism.* Hoboken, NJ: Jossey-Bass.

Altemeyer, B. (1996). *The authoritarian specter.* Cambridge, MA: Harvard University Press.

Altemeyer, B. (1998). The other "authoritarian personality". *Advances in Experimental Social Psychology, 30,* 47–92.

Bakker, B. N., Lelkes, Y., & Malka, A. (2021). Reconsidering the link between self-reported personality traits and political preferences. *American Political Science Review, 115*(4), 1482–1498.

Brown, K., Mondon, A., & Winter, A. (2023). The far right, the mainstream and mainstreaming: Towards a heuristic framework. *Journal of Political Ideologies, 28*(2), 162–179.

Brown, R. (1965). The authoritarian personality and the organization of attitudes. In R. Brown (Ed.), *Social psychology* (pp. 477–546). New York: Free Press.

Choma, B. L., & Hanoch, Y. (2017). Cognitive ability and authoritarianism: Understanding support for Trump and Clinton. *Personality and Individual Differences, 106*, 287–291.

Conway III, L. G., Houck, S. C., Gornick, L. J., & Repke, M. A. (2018). Finding the Loch Ness monster: Left-wing authoritarianism in the United States. *Political Psychology, 39* (5), 1049–1067.

Davis, D. W., & Silver, B. D. (2004). Civil liberties vs. security: Public opinion in the context of the terrorist attacks on America. *American Journal of Political Science, 48* (1), 28–46.

Doty, R. M., Peterson, B. E., & Winter, D. G. (1991). Threat and authoritarianism in the United States, 1978–1987. *Journal of Personality and Social Psychology, 61* (4), 629.

Duckitt, J., Wagner, C., Du Plessis, I., & Birum, I. (2002). The psychological bases of ideology and prejudice: Testing a dual process model. *Journal of Personality and Social Psychology, 83* (1), 75.

Duriez, B., & Van Hiel, A. (2002). The march of modern fascism. A comparison of social dominance orientation and authoritarianism. *Personality and Individual Differences, 32* (7), 1199–1213.

Engelhardt, A. M., Feldman, S., & Hetherington, M. J. (2023). Advancing the measurement of authoritarianism. *Political Behavior, 45*, 537–560.

Eysenck, H. J. (2018). *The psychology of politics*. London: Routledge. (Original work published 1954).

Feldman, S. (2003). Enforcing social conformity: A theory of authoritarianism. *Political Psychology, 24*, 41–74.

Feldman, S. (2020). Authoritarianism, threat, and intolerance. In E. Borgida, J. M. Federico, C. Miller, & J. L. Sullivan (Eds.), *At the forefront of political psychology: Essays in honor of John L. Sullivan*. London: Routledge.

Feldman, S., & Stenner, K. (1997). Perceived threat and authoritarianism. *Political Psychology, 18* (4), 741–770.

Fromm, E. (1994). *Escape from freedom*. New York: Henry Holt & Company. (Original work published in 1941).

Helminen, V., Wass, H., Kantola, A., & Elovainio, M. (2024). Nordic authoritarianism: Child-rearing values and political behavior in a multiparty context. *Political Psychology, 45* (1), 91–111.

Hetherington, M., & Suhay, E. (2011). Authoritarianism, threat, and Americans' support for the war on terror. *American Journal of Political Science, 55* (3), 546–560.

Jedinger, A., & Kaminski, S. (2024). The association between system-justifying ideologies and attitudes toward the social market economy in Germany. *Current Psychology, 43* (4), 3562–3572.

Luttig, M. D. (2021). Reconsidering the relationship between authoritarianism and Republican support in 2016 and beyond. *The Journal of Politics, 83* (2), 783–787.

McFarland, S. G., Ageyev, V. S., & Djintcharadze, N. (1996). Russian authoritarianism two years after communism. *Personality and Social Psychology Bulletin, 22* (2), 210–217.

Napier, J. L., & Jost, J. T. (2008). The "antidemocratic personality" revisited: A cross-national investigation of working-class authoritarianism. *Journal of Social Issues, 64* (3), 595–617.

Nilsson, A. (2024). Antidemocratic tendencies on the left, the right, and beyond: A critical review of the theory and measurement of left-wing authoritarianism. *Political Psychology*, *45* (4), 693–708.

Nilsson, A., & Jost, J. T. (2020). The authoritarian-conservatism nexus. *Current Opinion in Behavioral Sciences*, *34*, 148–154.

Peresman, A., Carroll, R., & Bäck, H. (2021). Authoritarianism and immigration attitudes in the UK. *Political Studies*, *71* (3), 616–633.

Pérez, E. O., & Hetherington, M. J. (2014). Authoritarianism in black and white: Testing the cross-racial validity of the child rearing scale. *Political Analysis*, *22* (3), 398–412.

Pratto, F., Sidanius, J., Stallworth, L. M., & Malle, B. F. (1994). Social dominance orientation: A personality variable predicting social and political attitudes. *Journal of Personality and Social Psychology*, *67* (4), 741.

Sales, S. M. (1973). Threat as a factor in authoritarianism: An analysis of archival data. *Journal of Personality and Social Psychology*, *28* (1), 44.

Shils, E. A. (1954). Authoritarianism right and left. In R. Christie & M. Jahoda (Eds.), *Studies in the scope and method of the authoritarian personality* (pp. 24–49). New York: Free Press.

Sidanius, J., Pratto, F., Van Laar, C., & Levin, S. (2004). Social dominance theory: Its agenda and method. *Political Psychology*, *25* (6), 845–880.

Stenner, K. (2005). *The authoritarian dynamic*. Cambridge: Cambridge University Press.

Stone, W. F. (1980). The myth of left-wing authoritarianism. *Political Psychology*, *2* (3/4), 3–19.

Van Hiel, A., Duriez, B., & Kossowska, M. (2006). The presence of left-wing authoritarianism in Western Europe and its relationship with conservative ideology. *Political Psychology*, *27* (5), 769–793.

Vasilopoulos, P., & Lachat, R. (2018). Authoritarianism and political choice in France. *Acta Politica*, *53* (4), 612–634.

Vasilopoulos, P., Marcus, G. E., & Foucault, M. (2018). Emotional responses to the Charlie Hebdo attacks: Addressing the authoritarianism puzzle. *Political Psychology*, *39* (3), 557–575.

Vasilopoulos, P., McAvay, H., Brouard, S., & Foucault, M. (2023). Emotions, governmental trust and support for the restriction of civil liberties during the covid-19 pandemic. *European Journal of Political Research*, *62* (2), 422–442.

Vasilopoulos, P., & Robinson, J. (2025). Authoritarianism, political attitudes, and vote choice: A longitudinal analysis of the British Electorate. *Political Behavior*, *47*, 503–527.

Chapter 4

Personality and Political Behavior

Introduction

Popular explanations on how citizens reach political choices very often entail a form of self-interest. Managerial classes and landowners tend to oppose wealth taxes as they limit their incomes Lower income people tend to be supportive of welfare policies because they benefit from them, while some workers tend to oppose mass migration because they feel that they are competing with immigrants for jobs. These explanations have merit and have been validated in political research (e.g., Hasenfeld & Rafferty, 1989). However, social groups are much more diverse in their political orientations than self-interest would suggest. Some managers appear in favor of higher taxation, poor people are often against benefits, while many working-class people are supportive of immigration. This suggests that our political attitudes cannot be solely explained on the basis of self-interest based on group membership, and that individual characteristics come into play when we make political choices. In the previous chapter we discussed two such psychological characteristics, Authoritarianism and Social Dominance Orientations, that account for political behavior beyond self-interest.

Both Authoritarianism and Social Dominance Orientation were identified and studied precisely because of their merit in explaining political choice and specifically their relevance to understanding prejudice and preference for authoritarian leaders. In this chapter, we continue the exploration of how personality characteristics are associated with political ideology and other political choices using an alternative approach. Instead of focusing on specific personality types that are directly relevant for understanding prejudice or support for the far right, we will identify key traits that make human personalities different from one another and assess how each of these traits are associated with ideology, political attitudes, and political participation.

Personality and Personality Traits

Personality can be defined as "a multifaceted, enduring, internal psychological structure" (Mondak et al., 2010, p. 86). **Personality traits** are long-term individual differences that provide broad behavioral tendencies. An example of a

DOI: 10.4324/9781003460084-6

Personality: A stable and multidimensional individual psychological orientation that guides behavior.

Personality traits: Long-term individual differences that affect behavior; the separate components of personality.

personality trait is extraversion: some people are extroverted and enjoy meeting new people, going to parties, or being members of different associations. Others are quieter and more reserved and instead their ideal evening is watching a film or reading a book at home. This broad orientation has deep-ranging effects on a number of diverse behaviors such as choice of study (Vedel, 2016) or music taste (Rentfrow & Gosling, 2003).

Two things merit attention when it comes to the association of personality and behavioral outcomes, whether political or not. First, personality is *generally* associated with behavior. For instance, whether the general trait of extraversion will lead to extroverted behavior depends on the social environment and the type of situations in which extroverts find themselves. An extrovert in a desert will not have the opportunity to display their extraversion. Second, few people are extremely extroverted or extremely introverted. Most score in the middle of the spectrum. This distribution is similar to all personality traits.

Personality traits are thought to be a product both of socialization and biological mechanisms. Our personality crystallizes during early adulthood, with limited susceptibility to change later in life. Exceptions are significant life changes, such as migrating to a culturally different country (e.g., Güngör et al., 2013) or different forms of prolonged hardship such as experiencing long-term unemployment (e.g., Boyce et al., 2015) that have been found to have an impact on personality.

Individual differences in personality characteristics are key to understanding why people support different ideologies, endorse diverse political attitudes, and vary in their levels of political engagement. In the rest of this chapter I present some of the most prominent personality dimensions that are associated with political behavior and discuss their applicability in different contexts.

The Big Five Model of Personality

Psychology since the 1950s has attempted to map out personality dimensions that would allow a taxonomy of long-term traits that make humans different from one another. While several categorizations of personality have been proposed, today the **Big Five model** is the most widely used and accepted typology of personality (Caprara & Vecchione, 2013; McCrae & Costa, 2008). The Big Five factors of personality measure "broad dispositions that are theorized to shape responses to the full range of stimuli people encounter in the world" (Gerber et al., 2011, p. 269). The model argues that a large number of psychological traits can be adequately summarized in five broad dimensions. Importantly, the Big Five model has received empirical support across contexts, as studies have found that these five dimensions of personality meaningfully summarize personality differences across nations, cultures, and languages (McCrae & Costa, 1997).

Big Five model of personality: A widely accepted taxonomy of personality consisting of five independent traits – Openness to New Experiences, Conscientiousness, Extraversion, Agreeableness, and Neuroticism.

The Big Five personality traits are broad and this is an advantage in terms of practicality. It would have been impossible to measure and discuss personality using a model of, say, a hundred different personality types. In the 1960s, when examining different self-reports and ratings of personality among different samples, researchers noticed five recurrent factors (Tupes & Christal, 1961/1992). In other words, they realized that dozens of personality differences could be reasonably summarized in just five dimensions. For example, traits such as curious, smart, artistic, and imaginative, even though they are not in any way synonymous, tend to co-occur in most humans to an extent that allows us to consider them as part of a common, broad personality trait, instead of treating them as separate traits. Importantly, the Big Five personality traits are independent. This means that if we know the score of a person on one trait we cannot predict their score on each of the other traits. That is to say, there is no correlation between the five personality traits.

The Big Five traits (sometimes referred to as the OCEAN model of personality because of the acronym that they form) are **Openness to New Experiences, Conscientiousness, Extraversion, Agreeableness,** and **Neuroticism** (the latter sometimes referred to by its opposite term, *Emotional Stability*).

Openness to Experience: A personality trait capturing the extent to which someone is imaginative, curious, creative, and open to new ideas and experiences.

Conscientiousness: A personality trait capturing one's levels of order, impulse control, and sense of obligation.

Extraversion: A personality trait describing the extent to which a person is energetic and outgoing.

Agreeableness: A personality trait reflecting the extent to which an individual is generous, kind, compassionate, and prefers social harmony to antagonism.

Neuroticism: A personality trait reflecting one's emotional instability and their tendency to experience negative emotions.

- Openness to New Experiences refers to "the breadth, depth, originality and complexity of an individual's mental and experiential life" (John & Srivastava, 1999, p. 121). People who score high in Openness are typically described as imaginative, original, curious, insightful, and creative (McCrae & John, 1992). Openness to Experience is associated with behaviors such as interest in travels, having numerous and diverse hobbies, and being knowledgeable of foreign cuisine (McCrae & Costa, 2008). It is also associated with a propensity for risk-taking manifested in behaviors such as drug or alcohol use (Flory et al., 2002).
- Conscientiousness captures the dimension of order, impulse control, and sense of obligation. Conscientious individuals tend to be hardworking, rigid, efficient, reliable, thorough, and precise (Caprara & Vecchione, 2013). They tend to think before taking actions, adhere to norms and rules, and are well organized (John & Srivastava, 1999). Conscientiousness is associated with efficiency, responsibility, or technical expertise (McCrae & Costa, 2008). Conscientious individuals generally perform better at work, tend to earn higher wages (e.g., Duckworth et al., 2012), and have also been found to live longer compared to those scoring low on the trait (Deary et al., 2010).
- The dimension of extraversion captures an "energetic approach to the social and material world" (John & Srivastava, 1999, p. 121). Extroverts tend to be energetic, optimistic, outgoing, and talkative. They have many friends, are members of different group organizations, and have a positive emotionality. They are more likely to study social sciences and choose professions that involve sociability (Vedel, 2016).
- Agreeableness refers to "a set of interrelated dispositions and characteristics, manifested as differences in being likable, pleasant, and harmonious in relation with others" (Graziano & Tobin, 2013, p. 347). It captures the extent to which one is tender-minded, empathetic, altruistic, and conflict-avoidant (Tobin & Graziano, 2020). Being forgiving, generous, polite, modest, and trusting are all adjectives that describe people high in agreeableness (John & Srivastava, 1999; McCrae & John, 1992).
- Neuroticism refers to the extent to which one is prone to experiencing negative emotions such as anxiety, depression, hostility, or sadness (John & Srivastava, 1999). It is associated with pessimism, sensitivity to criticism, and low self-esteem (McCrae & Costa, 2008). Neuroticism is also associated with numerous negative mental and physical health outcomes and is of major interest to clinical psychologists and physicians (Lahey, 2009).

The Big Five and Political Behavior

Since the 1990s, when the Big Five model was consolidated within mainstream political psychology, there has been a rich stream of studies that show that citizens' political orientations are dependent on their personality traits above and beyond social characteristics such as gender, income, education, or social class. In the study of political behavior, Openness to Experience and Conscientiousness are considered the most influential traits, though recent research has also highlighted the merit of the rest of the three traits, and especially agreeableness.

Openness to New Experiences has been repeatedly found to be associated with left-wing (or liberal in US terms) political orientations (Carney et al., 2008; Jost et al., 2003; Schoen & Schumann, 2007). In fact, being liberal is one of the items often asked in personality tests that aim at capturing Openness. The mechanism that connects the two is straightforward: those who score high in Openness to New Experiences are attracted by change and novelty. Hence, they are more likely to question tradition, which is a cornerstone of conservatism (Jost et al., 2003). Further, people who are open to experience are more likely to be welcoming of, rather than threatened by, people with a different cultural background, including immigrants, or those leading a non-conventional lifestyle, such as members of the LGBTQI+ community (Gerber et al., 2011). Openness has also been found to be associated with voting for left-wing parties in several countries, including the UK (Aidt & Rauh, 2018), France (Vasilopoulos & Jost, 2020), Germany (Schoen & Schumann, 2007), Italy, Spain, and Poland (Vecchione et al., 2011) as well as Democrats in the United States (Wang, 2016). Some scholars argue that those scoring high in Openness to New Experiences are more likely to question extant social hierarchies and endorse social change, and hence should also be more likely to endorse left-wing economic policies (Gerber et al., 2010), yet others posit that this association is more likely a byproduct of left-wing partisanship rather than representing a truly causal relationship (Johnston et al., 2017).

In addition to political preferences, studies have investigated whether Openness to New Experiences is also associated with political participation (Gerber et al., 2011; Ha et al., 2013; Mondak et al., 2010). Some studies do find a positive effect on some forms of participation that they attribute to the intellectual curiosity that is associated with Openness and increases motivation to learn about – and, in turn, participate in – politics (Mondak et al., 2010). Yet the effect is not found across countries (Weinschenk, 2017), nor does it cover all forms of participation (Mondak et al., 2010).

Conscientiousness, on the other hand, has consistently been found to be associated with conservative political orientations (Bakker, 2017; Carney et al., 2008; Jost, 2021; Jost et al., 2003). Conscientious individuals tend to be rigid, hardworking, organized, and achievement-seeking. These characteristics render them more inclined to support economically conservative policies through preferences for social stability and the endorsement of beliefs such as that hard work gets one ahead in life (Gerber et al., 2010). Further, rigidity, increased sense of order, rule following, and need for being in control are all characteristics which correlate with social conservatism (Jost, 2021). A large wave of research has found associations between conscientiousness and voting for center-right and far-right parties in Europe and the United States (Aidt & Rauh, 2018; Schoen & Schumann, 2007; Vecchione et al., 2011). Conscientiousness has been found to have an inconsistent effect on participation, depending on the activity. It is positively associated in instances when political participation is perceived as a duty, such as voting (Gallego & Oberski, 2012) and, in some studies, negatively with unconventional forms of participation such as protesting (Mondak et al., 2010, 2011).

In early studies that were mostly conducted in the United States, Agreeableness was found to have a weaker influence on political behavior. However, subsequent analyses have identified that it is a personality trait that also plays an important role in shaping political attitudes and behavior. Agreeable individuals score high in altruism, generosity, kindness, collectiveness, and tender-mindedness. These traits motivate them to protect socially vulnerable groups, such as immigrants or refugees, and at the same time favor economic policies aiming to reduce free-market inequality. Indeed, agreeableness has been found to be a potent predictor compared to the rest of the personality traits when it comes to positive attitudes toward immigrants and minorities (e.g., Freitag & Rapp, 2015; Gallego & Pardos-Prado, 2014). Regarding economic preferences, studies point to a clear association between agreeableness and left-wing orientations across contexts (Bakker, 2017; Fatke, 2017; Gerber et al., 2010; Schoen & Schumann, 2007). Research has also identified a link between being agreeable and voting for left-wing parties in Europe (Aidt & Rauh, 2018; Vecchione et al., 2011). Finally, a recent comparative study in Western Europe, the United States, and Venezuela found that citizens scoring low in agreeableness are more likely to find the divisive and aggressive discourse of populist candidates of the Left and Right more appealing and cast a vote for them (Bakker et al., 2021; see also Bakker et al., 2016), even though this has not been confirmed in the case of the Far Left in France (Vasilopoulos & Jost, 2020).

Neuroticism has been found to be associated with the endorsement of left-wing economic attitudes. The mechanism is that neurotic individuals are more sensitive to experiencing anxiety over the prospect of economic loss and are therefore motivated to find policies that reduce the risks associated with a free-market system more appealing (Gerber et al., 2011; Schoen & Schumann, 2007). Hence, they are more likely to support left-wing economic policies associated with a strong welfare state that guarantees for example public access to health or increased social benefits (Bakker, 2017; Gerber et al., 2011; Schoen & Schumann, 2007). In turn, neuroticism has been found in some studies to be associated with voting left-wing parties, even though the effect is weak compared to the rest of the Big Five traits (e.g., Aidt & Rauh, 2018).

Finally, research suggests that extraversion has a limited influence on political attitudes and choice. Still, some studies associate it with different forms of political participation, especially if they involve an element of sociability (Mondak et al., 2010). The mechanism is simple and involves the pleasure that extroverts receive from activities that entail sociability. Moreover, extraversion has been found to be associated with political discussion (Mondak & Halperin, 2008). That said, most studies find a null effect of extraversion on mainstream forms of political participation, such as electoral turnout (e.g., Ha et al., 2013).

Table 4.1 summarizes the relationship between the Big Five traits and political behavior.

Table 4.1 The Big Five and Political Behavior

	Description (John & Srivastava, 1999, p. 121)	*Adjectives (McCrae & John, 1992)*	*Key Associations with Political Behavior*
Openness to new experiences	"Breadth, depth, originality and complexity of an individual's mental and experiential life"	Artistic, curious, imaginative, insightful, innovative, creative, original	Left-wing ideological identification Positive attitudes toward immigration Voting for left-wing parties
Conscientiousness	"Socially prescribed impulse control that facilitates task and goal-directed behavior, such as thinking before acting, delaying gratification, following norms and rules, and planning, organizing and prioritizing tasks"	Efficient, concentrated, organized, responsible, precise, reliable	Right-wing ideological identification Conservative economic preferences Conservative social preferences Voting for right-wing parties
Extraversion	"An energetic approach to the social and material world"	Active, dynamic, sociable, enthusiastic, energetic, outgoing, talkative	No consistent effects
Agreeableness	"A pro-social and communal orientation toward others and includes traits such as altruism, tender-mindedness, trust and modesty"	Forgiving, generous, kind, modest, sympathetic, trusting	Negative association with support for populist candidates Positive attitudes toward immigration
Neuroticism	"Negative emotionality, such as feeling anxious, nervous, sad, and tense"	Anxious; self-pitying; tense; touchy; worrying; unstable	Preference for left-wing economic policies

Do Our Political Preferences Also Affect Our Personalities?

Most studies on the association between personality traits and political choice assume that personality is causally prior to our political attitudes. The argument is that personalities develop earlier in life compared to political attitudes and hence they should cause attitudes rather than the other way round (Verhulst et al., 2012). However, recent studies suggest that our political preferences may also affect our personality traits (e.g., Bakker et al., 2021). Bakker et al. explain their findings based on two broad reasons. The first is that people with similar political preferences tend to interact more frequently, fostering, for example, common norms and worldviews that may be expressed in aspects of their personality. The second mechanism is that people are aware of the stereotypical labels associated with their political ideology (e.g., compassionate liberals and tough conservatives, see Clifford, 2020) and express these tendencies when asked about their personalities. Hence, it is becoming increasingly accepted in political psychology that in addition to our personalities causing our political attitudes, our psychological characteristics may also be caused in part by our political preferences (see also Osborne et al., 2021; Vasilopoulos & Robinson, 2025).

Other Personality Traits: Need for Cognition and the Dark Triad

In addition to the Big Five, political psychologists have explored other psychological characteristics that are potentially useful for understanding the psychological motivations of political choice. Two such examples include **Need for Cognition** and the **Dark Triad.**

Need for cognition is a psychological trait that refers to the "tendency for people to vary in the extent to which they engage in and enjoy effortful cognitive activities" (Petty et al., 2009, p. 318l; see also Cacioppo & Petty, 1982). Those scoring high in need for cognition enjoy complexity, are more comfortable with being ambivalent, and are more receptive to information that challenges their preexisting conclusions (Arceneaux & Vander Wielen, 2013). Those scoring low tend to seek out a minimal amount of information to reach a conclusion, are uncomfortable with ambivalence, and more likely to engage in stereotypical thinking. In the realm of politics, those scoring high in need for cognition are more likely to read more complex news stories (Sohlberg, 2019) and more likely

> **Need for Cognition**: The extent to which people engage in and enjoy effortful cognitive endeavors.
>
> **Dark Triad**: Refers to the interconnected traits of Narcissism, Machiavellianism, and psychopathy.

to update their partisan preferences following exposure to negative information (Arceneaux & Vander Wielen, 2013). Furthermore, studies have found that conservatives are more likely to score low in need for cognition compared to left-wing citizens in different settings (Hennes et al., 2012; Jost, 2017; Jost et al., 2003).

More recently, research has explored how the so-called Dark Triad translates into differences in political orientations. The Dark Triad consists of three traits: the first is **Narcissism**, which refers to a tendency for grandiose fantasizing, antagonism, aggression, and a need to be admired (Cichocka et al., 2022). Second, **Machiavellianism** refers to a tendency toward devious, power-seeking, and manipulative behavior and is associated with lack of trust and an inclination to deceive others for personal gain (Chen et al., 2021). Finally, **Psychopathy** refers to callousness, manipulation, impulsive behavior, taking advantage of others, and low levels of anxiety and empathy (Hodson et al., 2009). These traits (which are all negatively associated with agreeableness, Hodson et al., 2009) have been found to influence political behavior above and beyond the Big Five. They are typically associated with prejudice toward outgroups and right-wing political orientations (Hodson et al., 2009; Moss & O'Connor, 2020). Narcissism is particularly useful for understanding susceptibility to conspiracy theories: paranoid beliefs of persecution, a need to blame others for the narcissist's own failures, and a need to feel unique (through having access to the information that powerful actors want to hide from the public) are all psychological mechanisms that render conspiracy theories appealing (Cichocka et al., 2022).

Narcissism: The tendency for grandiose fantasizing, antagonism, aggression, and a need to be admired.

Machiavellianism: A tendency toward devious, power-seeking, and manipulative behavior. It is associated with lack of trust and an inclination to deceive others for personal gain.

Psychopathy: A personality trait integrating callousness, manipulation, impulsive behavior, taking advantage of others, and low levels of anxiety and empathy.

Personality and Political Behavior: A Universal Relationship?

An important drawback on research on the Big Five and political orientations is that the vast majority of studies on the topic focus on Western, Educated, Industrialized, Rich, and Democratic (W.E.I.R.D.) countries, and we do not know if they apply to countries with different economic, social, and political systems (Bakker, 2023; Beattie et al., 2022). A few recent studies have sought to address this gap. In his investigation of the association between the Big Five traits and policy attitudes in a diverse set of 21 countries, both from the Global North and South, Fatke (2017) found that personality effects vary by country: Openness to New Experiences was strongly associated with left-wing social attitudes in liberal democracies, while agreeableness was associated with left-wing economic preferences in affluent, but not in poor, countries. In another important study Beattie and colleagues looked into the relationship between the Big Five and political orientations in China and found that conscientiousness was associated with support for the left rather than the right (2022). They attribute their finding to the specificities of the Chinese ideological spectrum where the one pole consists of a "conservative left" that in W.E.I.R.D terms would translate into a mix of social conservative and economic left-wing policies and the other pole consist of a "liberal right" that combines socially liberal and economically conservative values. Finally, in a large comparative study on the association of the Big Five with different forms of political participation in the global North and South, Weinschenk (2017) found significant discrepancies between countries. This finding could be attributed to differences in regime characteristics, the information environment, or aspects of national political cultures. In summary, these studies suggest that the patterns described in the previous section are not universal but conditional to the specific national context and more research is needed to better understand the personality substrates of political behavior in non-W.E.I.R.D contexts.

Conclusion

This chapter discussed the personality underpinnings of political choice. There is consensus among political psychology scholars that our personality structures correlate with political preferences and willingness to participate in politics. This has important implications for understanding political competition and deliberation in contemporary politics.

First, it helps us understand why it is sometimes impossible for people to agree on what constitutes desirable policy, no matter the goodwill for deliberation. Take the issue of immigration. Regardless of discussions on the benefits or harms of immigration, left-wing people (who tend to score high in Openness to New Experiences) are more likely to be psychologically structured to find living in a multicultural society inherently exciting because it brings opportunities to encounter heterogeneous cultures, customs, lifestyles, and languages. Conversely, right-wing individuals (who tend to score low in Openness to New Experiences) are more likely to feel discomfort or even threat when living in an ethnically diverse setting. Bridging these two orientations is difficult as disagreements are partly rooted in our most profound psychological substrates, our personalities.

The association between personality and political views also helps us understand a key development in many places around the world, which is the increasing dislike for people who support ideologically opposing parties (or "affective polarization" as political scientists call it). Hetherington and Weiler trace the root of the rise in divisions across partisan lines in the increasing convergence between personality and party identification (2018). Economic development and demographic change have gradually increased the salience of social issues in public discourse, such as gender, race, immigration, or sexual orientation (e.g., Inglehart, 1990). These are the types of issues that correspond more closely to our personality types, and especially the openness/closeness to experience dimension that is one of the most important in political behavior. As these issues become increasingly important, citizens decide which party to support on the basis of their personality traits. In other words, partisans are increasingly sorted into political parties in line with their personality characteristics: people who score high in openness are increasingly supporting left-wing parties and people who score low are increasingly supporting right-wing parties because of their attitudes on social issues (Hetherington & Weiler, 2018). This bears the consequence that a political cleavage becomes a personality cleavage, which creates animosity between partisans of left-wing and right-wing parties and has a deleterious effect on political tolerance and deliberation. Importantly, personality affects key social factors such as residential choice and enrolment in higher education: Openness is associated with attending university and a preference for living in urban centers, while closeness is associated with not attending university and living in rural areas. Hence many societies end up having partisan cleavages along these dimensions, which in turn further refuels affective polarization. This personality cleavage is also reflected in lifestyle and consumer choices, such as music, film, or food preferences.

At the same time personality provides a broad motivation to behavior, including political behavior. If politics was only about personality, there would not be fluctuations in political attitudes, party shares, or political participation. Numerous additional social, economic, and psychological factors are at play when we decide on political issues. I explore some of these in the next chapters.

Further Reading

https://openpsychometrics.org/tests/IPIP-BFFM/: Here you can try a Big Five personality test to see where you score on each of the five traits.

Jost, J. T. (2021). *Left and right: The psychological significance of a political distinction.* Oxford: Oxford University Press. Offers a thorough overview of research on the psychological differences between leftwing and rightwing voters.

Nai, A., & Maier, J. (2023). *Dark politics: The personality of politicians and the future of democracy.* Oxford: Oxford University Press. The authors extend research on personality and politics by investigating the Dark Triad traits among politicians in different countries.

References

Aidt, T., & Rauh, C. (2018). The Big Five personality traits and partisanship in England. *Electoral Studies*, *54*, 1–21.

Arceneaux, K., & Vander Wielen, R. J. (2013). The effects of need for cognition and need for affect on partisan evaluations. *Political Psychology*, *34* (1), 23–42.

Bakker, B. N. (2017). Personality traits, income, and economic ideology. *Political Psychology*, *38* (6), 1025–1041.

Bakker, B. N. (2023). Personality approaches to political behavior. In L. Huddy D. O. Sears, & J. S. Levy (Eds.), *The Oxford handbook of political psychology* (3rd ed., pp. 21–64). Oxford: Oxford University Press.

Bakker, B. N., Rooduijn, M., & Schumacher, G. (2016). The psychological roots of populist voting: Evidence from the United States, the Netherlands and Germany. *European Journal of Political Research*, *55* (2), 302–320.

Bakker, B. N., Schumacher, G., & Rooduijn, M. (2021). The populist appeal: Personality and antiestablishment communication. *The Journal of Politics*, *83* (2), 589–601.

Beattie, P., Chen, R., & Bettache, K. (2022). When left is right and right is left: The psychological correlates of political ideology in China. *Political Psychology*, *43* (3), 457–488.

Boyce, C. J., Wood, A. M., Daly, M., & Sedikides, C. (2015). Personality change following unemployment. *Journal of Applied Psychology*, *100* (4), 991.

Cacioppo, J. T., & Petty, R. E. (1982). The need for cognition. *Journal of Personality and Social Psychology*, *42* (1), 116.

Caprara, G. V., & Vecchione, M. (2013). Personality approaches to political behavior. In L. Huddy, D. O. Sears, & J. S. Levy (Eds.), *The Oxford handbook of political psychology* (pp. 23–58). Oxford: Oxford University Press.

Carney, D. R., Jost, J. T., Gosling, S. D., & Potter, J. (2008). The secret lives of liberals and conservatives: Personality profiles, interaction styles, and the things they leave behind. *Political Psychology*, *29* (6), 807–840.

Chen, P., Pruysers, S., & Blais, J. (2021). The dark side of politics: Participation and the Dark Triad. *Political Studies*, *69* (3), 577–601.

Cichocka, A., Marchlewska, M., & Biddlestone, M. (2022). Why do narcissists find conspiracy theories so appealing? *Current Opinion in Psychology*, (47), 101386.

Clifford, S. (2020). Compassionate democrats and tough republicans: How ideology shapes partisan stereotypes. *Political Behavior*, *42* (4), 1269–1293.

Deary, I. J., Weiss, A., & Batty, G. D. (2010). Intelligence and personality as predictors of illness and death: How researchers in differential psychology and chronic disease epidemiology are collaborating to understand and address health inequalities. *Psychological Science in the Public Interest*, *11* (2), 53–79.

Duckworth, A. L., Weir, D., Tsukayama, E., & Kwok, D. (2012). Who does well in life? Conscientious adults excel in both objective and subjective success. *Frontiers in Psychology*, *3*, 356.

Fatke, M. (2017). Personality traits and political ideology: A first global assessment. *Political Psychology*, *38* (5), 881–899.

Flory, K., Lynam, D., Milich, R., Leukefeld, C., & Clayton, R. (2002). The relations among personality, symptoms of alcohol and marijuana abuse, and symptoms of comorbid psychopathology: Results from a community sample. *Experimental and Clinical Psychopharmacology*, *10* (4), 425.

Freitag, M., & Rapp, C. (2015). The personal foundations of political tolerance towards immigrants. *Journal of Ethnic and Migration Studies*, *41* (3), 351–373.

Gallego, A., & Oberski, D. (2012). Personality and political participation: The mediation hypothesis. *Political Behavior*, *34*, 425–451.

Gallego, A., & Pardos-Prado, S. (2014). The big five personality traits and attitudes towards immigrants. *Journal of Ethnic and Migration Studies*, *40* (1), 79–99.

Gerber, A. S., Huber, G. A., Doherty, D., & Dowling, C. M. (2011). The big five personality traits in the political arena. *Annual Review of Political Science*, *14*, 265–287.

Gerber, A. S., Huber, G. A., Doherty, D., Dowling, C. M., & Ha, S. E. (2010). Personality and political attitudes: Relationships across issue domains and political contexts. *American Political Science Review*, *104* (1), 111–133.

Graziano, W. G., & Tobin, R. M. (2013). Agreeableness as an integrated process of cognition and emotion. In M. D. Robinson, E. Watkins, & E. Harmon-Jones (Eds.), *Handbook of cognition and emotion* (pp. 347–364). New York: Guilford.

Güngör, D., Bornstein, M. H., De Leersnyder, J., Cote, L., Ceulemans, E., & Mesquita, B. (2013). Acculturation of personality: A three-culture study of Japanese, Japanese Americans, and European Americans. *Journal of Cross-Cultural Psychology*, *44* (5), 701–718.

Ha, S. E., Kim, S., & Jo, S. H. (2013). Personality traits and political participation: Evidence from South Korea. *Political Psychology*, *34* (4), 511–532.

Hasenfeld, Y., & Rafferty, J. A. (1989). The determinants of public attitudes toward the welfare state. *Social Forces*, *67* (4), 1027–1048.

Hennes, E. P., Nam, H. H., Stern, C., & Jost, J. T. (2012). Not all ideologies are created equal: Epistemic, existential, and relational needs predict system-justifying attitudes. *Social Cognition*, *30* (6), 669–688.

Hetherington, M., & Weiler, J. (2018). *Prius or pickup?: How the answers to four simple questions explain America's great divide*. Boston, MA: Houghton Mifflin.

Hodson, G., Hogg, S. M., & MacInnis, C. C. (2009). The role of "dark personalities" (narcissism, Machiavellianism, psychopathy), Big Five personality factors, and ideology in explaining prejudice. *Journal of Research in Personality*, *43* (4), 686–690.

Inglehart, R. (1990). *Culture shift in advanced industrial society*. Princeton, NJ: Princeton University Press.

John, O. P., & Srivastava, S. (1999). The Big Five trait taxonomy: History, measurement, and theoretical perspectives. In L. A. Pervin & O. P. John (Eds.), *Handbook of personality: Theory and research* (pp. 102–138). New York: The Guilford Press.

Johnston, C. D., Lavine, H. G., & Federico, C. M. (2017). *Open versus closed: Personality, identity, and the politics of redistribution*. Cambridge: Cambridge University Press.

Jost, J. T. (2017). Ideological asymmetries and the essence of political psychology. *Political Psychology*, *38* (2), 167–208.

Jost, J. T., Glaser, J., Kruglanski, A. W., & Sulloway, F. J. (2003). Political conservatism as motivated social cognition. *Psychological Bulletin*, *129* (3), 339.

Lahey, B. B. (2009). Public health significance of neuroticism. *American Psychologist*, *64* (4), 241.

McCrae, R. R., & Costa, P. T. (1997). Personality trait structure as a human universal. *American Psychologist*, *52* (5), 509.

McCrae, R. R., & Costa, P. T., Jr. (2008). The five-factor theory of personality. In O. P. John, R. W. Robins, & L. A. Pervin (Eds.), *Handbook of personality: Theory and research*. New York: The Guilford Press.

McCrae, R. R., & John, O. P. (1992). An introduction to the five-factor model and its applications. *Journal of Personality, 60* (2), 175–215.

Mondak, J. J., Canache, D., Seligson, M. A., & Hibbing, M. V. (2011). The participatory personality: Evidence from Latin America. *British Journal of Political Science, 41* (1), 211–221.

Mondak, J. J., & Halperin, D. K. (2008). A framework for the study of personality and political behaviour. *British Journal of Political Science, 38* (2), 335–362.

Mondak, J. J., Hibbing, M. V., Canache, D., Seligson, M. A., & Anderson, M. R. (2010). Personality and civic engagement: An integrative framework for the study of trait effects on political behavior. *American Political Science Review, 104* (1), 85–110.

Moss, J., & O'Connor, P. J. (2020). The Dark Triad traits predict authoritarian political correctness and alt-right attitudes. *Heliyon, 6* (7), e04453.

Osborne, D., Satherley, N., Little, T. D., & Sibley, C. G. (2021). Authoritarianism and social dominance predict annual increases in generalized prejudice. *Social Psychological and Personality Science, 12* (7), 1136–1145.

Petty, R. E., Brinol, P., Loersch, C., & McCaslin, M. J. (2009). The need for cognition. In M. R. Leary & R. H. Hoyle (Eds.), *Handbook of individual differences in social behavior* (pp. 318–329). New York: The Guilford Press.

Rentfrow, P. J., & Gosling, S. D. (2003). The do re mi's of everyday life: The structure and personality correlates of music preferences. *Journal of Personality and Social Psychology, 84* (6), 1236.

Schoen, H., & Schumann, S. (2007). Personality traits, partisan attitudes, and voting behavior. Evidence from Germany. *Political Psychology, 28* (4), 471–498.

Sohlberg, J. (2019). Elections are (not) exciting: Need for cognition and electoral behaviour. *Scandinavian Political Studies, 42* (2), 138–150.

Tobin, R. M., & Graziano, W. G. (2020). Agreeableness. In Carducci, B. J., Nave, C.S., Mio, J.S., & Riggio, R.E. (Eds.), *The Wiley encyclopedia of personality and individual differences: Models and theories* (pp. 105–110). Hoboken, NJ: Wiley

Tupes, E. C., & Christal, R. E. (1961/1992). Recurrent personality factors based on trait ratings. *Journal of Personality, 60* (2), 225–251.

Vasilopoulos, P., & Jost, J. T. (2020). Psychological similarities and dissimilarities between left-wing and right-wing populists: Evidence from a nationally representative survey in France. *Journal of Research in Personality, 88*, 104004.

Vasilopoulos, P., & Robinson, J. (2025). Authoritarianism, political attitudes, and vote choice: A longitudinal analysis of the British Electorate. *Political Behavior, 47* (2), 503–527.

Vecchione, M., Schoen, H., Castro, J. L. G., Cieciuch, J., Pavlopoulos, V., & Caprara, G. V. (2011). Personality correlates of party preference: The Big Five in five big European countries. *Personality and Individual Differences, 51* (6), 737–742.

Vedel, A. (2016). Big Five personality group differences across academic majors: A systematic review. *Personality and Individual Differences, 92*, 1–10.

Verhulst, B., Eaves, L. J., & Hatemi, P. K. (2012). Correlation not causation: The relationship between personality traits and political ideologies. *American Journal of Political Science, 56* (1), 34–51.

Wang, C. H. (2016). Personality traits, political attitudes and vote choice: Evidence from the United States. *Electoral Studies, 44*, 26–34.

Weinschenk, A. C. (2017). Big five personality traits, political participation, and civic engagement: Evidence from 24 countries. *Social Science Quarterly, 98* (5), 1406–1421.

Chapter 5

Intragroup Dynamics

Norms, Conformity, and Obedience

Introduction

In the previous two chapters, we discussed research on the relationship between individual psychological characteristics and political preferences. However, individuals do not exist in isolation. They continuously interact with friends, family, coworkers, or strangers as they go about their daily lives. This chapter investigates the ways in which our judgment and behavior are influenced by our social environment. Much of the exciting research on social influence that we will cover in the following pages may seem counterintuitive. This is because we tend to consider ourselves as autonomous actors who reach all sorts of decisions through independent thinking. For example, we have our own music and personal clothing style that reflects our individuality. We have our favorite foods, brands, language expressions, and habits. We even have our own "unpopular opinions" that we share on social media, only to discover that many others share the exact same ones. And of course, we support policies based on what *we* think is best for the country.

At the same time many of us are aware – or at least suspect – that social influence plays a role in behavior, yet we see it more clearly in others than ourselves. A series of fascinating experiments by psychologist Emily Pronin and her colleagues demonstrated that while we readily attribute others' behaviors to social influence, we tend to attribute our own choices to our autonomous judgments rather than to the influence of those around us (Pronin et al., 2007). Social influence is, however, an inescapable aspect of our human condition. It affects others and ourselves. We observe the views and behaviors of our peers, and we adjust ours accordingly, either consciously or unconsciously. As we shall see later in this chapter, political behavior is no exception.

Social psychologists discovered the influence of the social environment on individual behaviors early on. Research on social influence covers a timespan of more than nine decades, having produced a very rich literature showing how social forces affect our social and political beliefs and actions. This chapter will

DOI: 10.4324/9781003460084-7

Social norms: Informal, unwritten rules describing acceptable and unacceptable behaviors.

focus on a number of fundamental theories that are considered classic in the field and then discuss their significance for understanding the psychology of political behavior. It begins with an overview of research on the development and consolidation of **social norms** – or in other words – the unwritten rules of acceptable conduct and how these matter for understanding contemporary politics.

Social Norms

Social norms refer to "stereotypic perceptions, beliefs, and modes of conduct associated with a group" (Hogg & Abrams, 1988, p. 140). They are informal rules around appropriate behaviors, beliefs, and actions within society as a whole or within the context of a particular social group. We continuously draw on norms to guide our behavior in our everyday social life, most of the time without realizing. For example, when we are at a quiet beach we do not place our towel right next to a person we don't know. This would violate norms around personal intimacy. Other examples of social norms are that we address elderly people with respect or that we feel an obligation to repay someone who has provided us with a benefit. These norms are broadly shared across most societies. However, norms may vary across cultures due to different rules on how people ought to behave. The difference in norms is easier to realize when traveling abroad or living in another country. I can speak from personal experience as a Greek living in the UK. One of the many differences in norms between the two countries is that arriving late at a social occasion in the UK is considered rude whereas in Greece arriving on time would be seen as rather unusual. Sometimes norms change along with context: while it is entirely inappropriate to shout in a lecture theater, it is fully acceptable in the context of a football game.

Norms are forged and reproduced within social groups and sometimes function as differentiators between groups (Hogg & Abrams, 1988). For instance, members of a particular social class develop common behavioral repertoires (e.g., Kraus et al., 2012) that differentiate them from other social classes. Being subtle, reserved, articulate, and emotionally disengaged are often recognized as behavioral norms of the upper classes. Such norms often provide signals of the class background of a person. Finally, norms change over time. Modes of conduct that were deemed appropriate a few decades back are now unacceptable. This becomes evident when we watch old series or films and observe behaviors that may seem odd, or even repulsive, to us.

Social psychology has researched the development and consolidation of social norms since the early 20th century. Norms bear an important significance for our political behavior. People learn from a young age which beliefs and behaviors are socially encouraged and acceptable and which are socially stigmatized and unacceptable. A classic example concerns the political views we are willing to express. For instance, when responding to surveys many people may refrain from expressing overtly racist or sexist views as they understand that this would violate core social norms. As we analyze in more detail later in this chapter our norms develop by interacting with others and by monitoring our social environment for behaviors that are deemed appropriate and behaviors that are socially sanctioned. Because of this constant monitoring norms are prone to change. But before turning to that, we start with a simple question: How do social groups develop homogenous beliefs?

The Development of Norms – Sherif's Autokinetic Experiment

Muzafer Sherif, a Turkish American social psychologist, was one of the first to conduct research on how norms develop (1936). His experiments drew on what is called the "autokinetic phenomenon". This is a phenomenon that involves our visual perception: when humans are shown a point of light in a dark environment they tend to mistakenly perceive it as moving even though it remains still. This happens because our brains perceive motion in relation to a reference point and the absence of such a point creates the illusion of movement. Sherif took advantage of this phenomenon to investigate how people make judgments of ambiguous stimuli and whether – within the context of a group – people would coordinate to form a common judgment.

He conducted experiments where participants were shown such a point of light and subsequently asked to estimate the distance of the supposed movement. There were two stages in these experiments. In the first, each participant was alone in a dark room. Sherif told them that a light would appear and after a short time it would start to move. The task was to estimate the distance the object had moved in inches. The experiment was repeated multiple times in the course of two days. Sherif discovered that participants' answers fell within a subjective range of distance, which was unique for each individual. In this stage, these individual responses were very different from one another. In the second stage, each participant repeated the same procedure in a group that consisted of two to three participants. It was this second stage that was mostly of interest to Sherif. He hypothesized, and confirmed, that in the context of the group, the answers in each replication would start to converge toward a group mean. Participants gradually abandoned their individual judgments to form a common judgment based on the estimations of those around them and, interestingly, would not admit that the group had any influence in their estimations. When they were called for a third time, this time individually, to estimate the distance of the light the participants reported similar distances to the ones that were collectively estimated within the group context. According to Sherif, participants had developed a social norm, which once developed, affected subsequent individual judgments. The theoretical significance of his work was that he showed that social groups tend to have a "binding power that locked individuals into their judgments" (Abrams & Levine, 2012, p. 7).

Norms and Social Conformity – The Asch Line Experiment

Sherif's work was ground-breaking as it cleverly illustrated that our individual judgments are shaped by others. But how does social influence work and why is it so effective? And how are norms internalized and solidified? To answer these questions, we need to take a closer look at studies investigating conformity. Salomon Asch, a Polish-American psychologist, conducted a series of fascinating experiments showing the power of **social conformity** (1951). These studies typically took place in the following way: participants were invited to take part in a scientific experiment on visual judgment. They were informed that they would be comparing the length of lines. In a room, a group of around six to eight people were shown two whiteboards. The one on the left showed one vertical black line and the one on the right three vertical black lines. The lines on the right panel were clearly different in length, such as the ones presented in Figure 5.1. All people in the room were asked to say in turn which of the lines on the right side was of equal length to the line on the left side. The answer in the example presented in the figure is, of course, C.

Social conformity: The tendency to adjust one's attitudes and behaviors based on those of the social group.

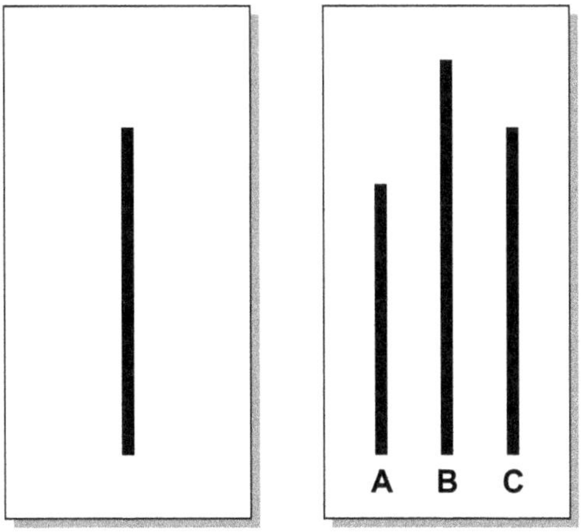

Figure 5.1 Sets of lines similar to those used by Asch (1955).

What the study subjects did not know was that this was not a test of vision but of conformity. In each group there was only one true study participant. This person always spoke last, that is after having heard the responses of everyone else. The rest of the group were Asch's confederates who were instructed to answer in a specific way each time. In most rounds they were providing the correct answer, yet in some rounds they had been instructed to unanimously give a wrong answer. Asch's aim was to see what the only actual study participant would answer when confronted with the wrong answers of the rest of the group. In other words, he was interested in discovering the impact of group pressure on conformity. The findings were counterintuitive: on average 35 per cent of the real participants gave the wrong answer under conditions of group pressure.

Asch tested multiple variations of the experiment. When only one real subject was pitted against one confederate he found that almost all true participants gave correct answers. When the opposition increased to two confederates and one true participant, 14 per cent gave the wrong answer. In a group of three confederates and one true subject the respective percentage increased to 32 per cent (Asch, 1955). The experiment has since been repeated multiple times across contexts and using different variations, with the results replicating consistently (Franzen & Mader, 2023; Takano & Sogon, 2008).

Two important questions in the Asch line experiments merit our attention: *Who* is more prone to giving wrong answers and *why*? Regarding the first question, research has established that people who score low on Openness to Experience – who are less likely to engage in independent thought (Franzen & Mader, 2023, see also Chapter 4) – are more vulnerable to social pressure. Similarly, those with a stronger need for social approval (Costanzo, 1970) are more likely to end up giving erroneous answers. As to *why* people give the wrong answer, Asch himself noticed different motivations (1955). Some *convert* (Crisp et al., 2024): they are genuinely convinced that what the majority says is correct, or in other words, they trust others more than their own perceptions. Others *comply* (Crisp et al., 2024): they conform publicly in order not to be exposed to disagreement, while privately they know that the majority is wrong.

Social Influence and Political Behavior

Political psychologists are particularly interested in studying norms and conformity as they help us understand multiple aspects of political behavior. For instance, there exists a large literature showing that different forms of social pressure bear an important impact on different forms of political participation across contexts (e.g., Bimber & De Zúñiga, 2022; Blais et al., 2019; Coulombe et al., 2024; Green & Gerber, 2019). Some studies show that when people are informed that their voting participation record may be in public display (as is the case with the United States) they tend to participate more (Gerber et al., 2008; Green & Gerber, 2019). The explanation is that electoral participation is a social norm in democracies, and that a public exposure of its violation may make abstentionists experience shame (see also Blais, 2000). Further, when people are shown evidence over their neighbors' electoral participation they become more likely to turn out in elections (e.g., Gerber et al., 2008; Green & Gerber, 2019).

Others have used theories of social norms to explain the mainstreaming of authoritarian leaders and parties in different contexts. The Asch experiment tells us an important story for understanding political behavior. We have a strong tendency to conform to the opinions of those around us. When we form an attitude on a policy, we are not only motivated to come up with an answer that best reflects our beliefs and values but we are also attentive to what other people around us think. This is because we trust the opinions of other people but also because we do not want to isolate ourselves from our social environment. This has important ramifications for understanding political behavior. There have been studies similar to the Asch line experiment where participants are called to express their political attitudes on the issue after they have heard a number of confederates unanimously supporting a specific political choice (Franzen & Mader, 2023). These studies clearly demonstrate social pressure effects on political attitudes.

A German political psychologist, Elizabeth Noelle-Neuman, further extended the premises of the Asch experiments to the realm of political behavior. In her **Spiral of Silence Theory** (1974, 1993), she famously argued that "to the individual, not isolating himself is more important than his own judgment" (1974, p. 43). Noelle-Neumann argues that people constantly monitor their social environment, observing which political opinions are on the rise and which ones are losing ground. In the first instance, people will be confident to express themselves "with an untroubled mind and without any danger of isolation" (1974, p. 44). However, when people perceive their ideas as declining they avoid expressing their opinions in order to avoid social isolation, thus triggering a spiral of silence: "The tendency of the one to speak up and the other to be silent starts off a spiraling process which increasingly established one opinion as the prevailing one" (Noelle-Neumann, 1974, p. 44). The spiral exclusively concerns *moral* issues, having to do for example with immigration, race, or LGBTQ rights. The mass media are pivotal in creating the spiral of silence as they provide information on which attitudes are on the rise and which are in

Spiral of Silence Theory: A public opinion theory suggesting that individuals monitor their social environment to assess which political attitudes are acceptable and which are stigmatized, adjusting their own political behavior accordingly.

decline. The media, according to Noelle-Neumann, tend to pass similar messages on behaviors and attitudes that are on the rise and socially acceptable. Her argument was that since journalists tend to be more liberal compared to the average citizen, conservative views on moral issues are perceived as being unacceptable or in decline.

Theories of norms, conformity, and the spiral of silence help us in understanding a worrying trend that we see across contexts: the mainstreaming of radical right ideas and candidates. Anti-prejudice norms, which were firmly embedded across countries until recently (Blinder et al., 2013), seem to be eroding. Consequently, prejudiced behaviors and attitudes that were not long ago stigmatized are becoming normalized. There is much research studying this process of norm change. For instance, Bursztyn and their colleagues (2020) show how norms can change swiftly when people perceive that their violation becomes increasingly acceptable in society. They argued that, following Trump's victory in the 2016 US election, Americans became more willing to express xenophobic views or at least consider them socially acceptable. This shift operates similarly to the dynamics seen in the Asch conformity experiment and the Spiral of Silence Theory: as people perceived that xenophobic attitudes were widely shared – signaled by Trump's popularity and eventual electoral win – they felt less social pressure to restrain themselves from expressing these views, while others became less inclined to criticize or sanction those who did. Valentim draws on theories of norms and conformity to reach a similar conclusion (2024). In line with the Spiral of Silence Theory, he argues that radical right mainstreaming is driven by citizens who already held radical right beliefs but were reluctant to express them as anti-prejudice norms were particularly dominant in the social sphere. Electoral successes of far-right parties or candidates (which may be attributable to exogenous factors) signal to the voters with concealed far-right preferences that their beliefs are now destigmatized, fueling these ideas into the mainstream (see also Box 5.1).

Box 5.1 How Mainstream Politicians Erode Norms (Valentim et al., 2025)

In a recent study, Valentim et al. (2025) cleverly illustrated how swift norm erosion can be, drawing on the case of Germany. In their study, they picked quotes on the issue of immigration and ethnic minority rights by politicians of the mainstream right (*Christian Democratic Union*) and the far right (*Alternative for Germany*) that were very similar in tone and content. They showed these quotes to different groups of participants. Since the message content was the same, the researchers were able to assess the impact of the message source (that is, *who* said the statement, rather than the statement itself) on behavior. First, they measured the direct impact of the messages on agreeing with xenophobic statements, the willingness to sign a hypothetical petition demanding a reduction in immigration from Afghanistan, and the willingness to report a tweet containing racist slurs targeting Muslims. Then, they asked respondents how they thought other people would assess these behaviors. They found that when xenophobic messages came with a mainstream right politician as a source, they were more effective in breaching anti-prejudice norms among respondents, compared to when the same message had a far-right politician as a source. Further, when the message had a center-right politician as a source, participants perceived the message as more popular and more appropriate. Valentim et al.'s research is fully in line with the conformity theories of Asch and Noelle-Neumann that we described in the previous section: mainstream center-right politicians are perceived as more popular compared to their far-right counterparts, signifying to the electorate what others think on a topic. Further, mainstream parties "occupy a more prestigious position as guardians of democratic norms because they often cite themselves as sharing values and norms of the establishment" (Valentim et al., 2025, p. 8). Hence, they are in a stronger position to change norms compared to parties that are on the outskirts of the party system and seen as extremist. These conclusions are alarming as they show that key democratic norms are subject to erosion when mainstream politicians undermine them.

Obedience: The Milgram Experiment

As described in the previous section, we have the tendency to conform by adjusting our behaviors and attitudes after observing those around us. An alternative form of compliance is **obedience**, which refers to compliance with direct commands coming from people with positions of power. In other words, whereas conformity refers to implicit compliance, obedience refers to explicit compliance with an order coming from a figure of authority (Crisp et al., 2024). For example, implicit compliance refers to observing your fellow students and following the social norm that students do not speak loudly in the library. Explicit compliance refers to remaining silent in the library after you have been told off by a member of staff. Research on obedience was inspired by the Nazi atrocities committed during the Second World War. Social psychologists of the time were interested in understanding the human capacity for cruelty as well as the psychological mechanisms behind it.

Obedience: Compliance based on direct commands by an authority figure.

The most seminal study on obedience is the infamous Milgram experiment (1963, 1974). Milgram was deeply influenced by Asch's work. He was interested in extending Asch's findings by testing whether following orders by established authorities (a recurring defense narrative among Nazi war criminals) could "induce a person to act with severity against another person" (Evans, 1976 – cited in Benjamin & Simpson, 2009, p. 13). With this purpose in mind he recruited 40 subjects from the area of New Haven, Connecticut in the United States through newspaper advertisements. The participants believed they were taking part in a study on memory and learning. They were paid a small amount just for coming to the laboratory and they could opt out at any point and still keep the money. The participant would arrive and meet with one of Milgram's accomplices to decide with the flip of a coin who would take the place of "teacher" and "learner" in the experiment. The selection process was rigged: participants always ended up taking the role of the teacher. Then the teacher and the learner were placed in separate rooms. The teacher was instructed by another actor who played the role of the experimenter (and hence the authority figure in the room) to administer electric shocks whenever the learner gave a wrong answer in a word-pairing exercise. The shocks increased in intensity with every wrong answer. The electric shock machine that the teacher handled had switches that clearly described the intensity of the administered shock, starting with slight (15 volts), moderate, strong, very strong, intense, extreme intensity, severe, and XXX (450 volts). As a point of reference most plugs around the world provide 230 volts. The experimenter's role was to instruct the teacher to continue administering the shocks, even when (in some versions of the experiment) they could hear the learner from the other room asking to stop, screaming in pain, or falling totally silent – the latter indicating that they may have actually passed unconscious or died as a result of the shocks. In reality, of course, the teacher was not administering any shocks, but participants believed that they did.

Before conducting his experiment, Milgram provided the details of his intended experiment with 14 senior psychology students asking them to predict how many participants would go on to inflict the maximum electric shock. Their estimates ranged from 0 to 3 per cent (Milgram, 1963). The actual number in the original experiment was 26 out of 40 or 65 per cent. This percentage is undoubtedly disturbing. But how is it possible? The participants were not sadistic individuals who enjoyed inflicting pain, of course. Besides, the experiment has since been replicated yielding similar results (Burger, 2009). The percentage was surprising to everyone (including Milgram) as the norm of not hurting others is deeply embedded in society, taught from a very young age. Indeed, most participants were in severe distress during the experiment, to the extent that it makes the Milgram experiment particularly problematic when it comes to research ethics (Benjamin & Simpson, 2009). In Milgram's words, "subjects were observed to sweat, tremble, stutter, bite their lips, groan, and dig their fingernails into

their flesh" (1963, p. 375). Many objected and made it clear they did not want to inflict pain on the learner, only to continue when instructed again by the authority figure. Instead of deciding on the basis of their own values and convictions, participants turned into "compliant automations willingly enacting the apparently obvious evil and destructive desires not by adoption of the aims of those giving the orders, but even more disturbing, by merely following instructions" (Marcus, 2013, p. 147).

The experiment forced participants to choose between two incompatible demands. The first was to avoid harming the learner and the other to obey the authority figure that instructed them to do so. The experiment shows that under pressure from authority figures people are willing to abandon their individual judgment, and eventually even their own morality. At a broader level, Milgram's experiment teaches us that under some circumstances our human autonomy may vanish. What were these circumstances in the specific experiment? According to Milgram, it was that, among else, the experiment was carried out by Yale, an authoritative, high status university, the goal of the experiment was a benevolent one (advancing science), the learner gave their initial consent to participate, and the participants were assured that the experiment was "painful but not dangerous" (even though the latter was intentionally contradicted by the labels in the electric shock board).

Milgram ran several variations of his experiment, helping us understand the psychological mechanism of obedience (1974 – see also Blass, 1991). For instance, not a single subject gave the maximum electric shock in variations where the experimenter called for a stop to the experiment but the victim wanted to continue or where there were two experimenters in the room and one asked for the experiment to stop. On the other hand, compliance was also affected by the degree of proximity to the victim. When the participant could see the victim being supposedly electrocuted, 40 per cent of participants gave the maximum shock. When the participant had to place the hand of the victim on a shock plate, full obedience fell to 30 per cent. All in all, these variations show that full obedience to the Milgram experiment is affected considerably more by variations in the authority figure rather than efforts to maximize proximity and empathy with the suffering victim.

The Banality of Evil

In 1961, the same time that Milgram was conducting his infamous experiments, the German-American Jewish philosopher Hannah Arendt was attending the trial of Adolf Eichmann, one of the most important trials of the 20th century, reporting on the six-month proceedings for *The New Yorker* magazine. The trial's importance lay in Eichmann's role as one of the principal organizers of the Holocaust. His role was of particular significance: as a high-ranking bureaucrat, he was responsible for the logistics of the mass extermination of six million Jews.

Banality of evil: The idea that evil is often committed by ordinary people who unthinkingly obey authority.

In 1960 Eichmann was abducted by the Israeli intelligence services in Argentina and was brought to trial in Israel. His trial attracted much publicity around the world. Unlike the Nuremberg trials, Eichmann's trial was broadcasted internationally so mass publics had detailed recounts of the atrocity of the Holocaust. Understandably, Eichmann should have been a disturbingly evil figure with psychopathic tendencies that enabled him to commit humanity's biggest crime. Yet this is not what Arendt saw. She perceived Eichmann as an ordinary, bland, and simple man who "never realized what he was doing" (2006, p. 287). She argued that his primary motivation for perpetrating the Final Solution had little to do with psychopathy or even an active hatred for Jews. Instead, the motivations were rather ordinary and *banal*, involving a desire for social acceptance and a strong ambition for professional advancement. The best word that characterized Eichmann's actions was *thoughtlessness*. Much as the subjects in Milgram's experiment, Eichmann, according to Arendt, was an unreflective bureaucratic operator in an environment that "created confusion over elementary questions of morality" and "the whole of respectable society had in one way or another succumbed to Hitler" (p. 295). These qualities led Arendt to develop her famous **banality of evil** concept. It refers to the idea that evil acts are not necessarily committed by sadistic, psychopathic, or otherwise abnormal actors. Many times, they arise from the routinized, mundane actions of everyday people who are obedient to authority without realizing the moral implications of their actions (2006). This is fully in line with the conclusions of the Milgram experiment.

Arendt's work has received a fair share of criticism that has predominantly focused on the accuracy of her portrayal of Eichmann. Subsequent historical accounts have refuted the claim that Eichmann was a mere operator, showing that he was in fact a fanatic anti-Semite who consciously endorsed and supported the Nazi ideology (see Cesarani, 2005). Others add nuance to the claim that individuals undergo an Eichmann-style behavioral transformation within the context of obedience to authority. They argue instead that psychological predispositions do play a role on who ends up inflicting evil and who does not under conditions of social pressure (Haslam & Reicher, 2007). That said, as is the case with the Milgram experiment, Arendt's argument spurred a long-lasting debate in political psychology over the power of situational circumstances on our behavior and the banality of evil is considered a key concept in the field.

Conclusion

This chapter explored key theories on the role that people around us play in our judgment and behavior. The theories around social norms, conformity, and obedience that we discussed point to the conclusion that our social environment has a strong – and sometimes dramatic – impact on our behavior. This comes at the expense of the influence of our individual traits, our judgment, and our moral values. In Milgram's own words: "The social psychology of this century reveals a major lesson: often it is not so much the kind of person a man is as the kind of situation in which he finds himself that determines how he will act" (1974, p. 205).

The legacy of these pioneering works on social influence and the academic discussion they generated, led to the reconceptualization of human behavior – and political behavior in particular – as an interaction between personality dispositions and the momentary context (Benjamin & Simpson, 2009). That is, social and political psychologists understand behavioral outcomes as a combination of our long-term personality traits and the situation we find ourselves in (e.g., Feldman & Stenner, 1997). Under situations where there is increased social pressure in the form of norms, majority opinion, or demands from positions of authority, our personalities will matter much less in predicting our actions. For example, the majority of the participants in the Milgram experiment acted as authoritarians without necessarily having an authoritarian personality. Overall, despite the illusion that we have an autonomy of judgment and action we are swayed by the attitudes and behaviors of those around us. Theories of social influence bear important implications for understanding a diverse set of political actions including the mass endorsement of authoritarian leaders and policies that is once again relevant in our modern era.

Further Reading

Arendt, H. (2006). *Eichmann in Jerusalem: A report on the Banality of Evil.* London: Penguin Books. Arendt's classic work on obedience and individual morality. (Original work published in 1963).

Lumet, S. (Director). (1957). *12 Angry Men* [Film]. United Artists. A classic film depicting group conformity and minority influence.

Noelle-Neumann, E. (1974). The spiral of silence a theory of public opinion. *Journal of Communication, 24* (2), 43–51. A concise presentation of the Spiral of Silence Theory and its implications.

Valentim, V. (2024). *The normalization of the radical right: A norms theory of political supply and demand.* Oxford: Oxford University Press. A fascinating study explaining the rise of the far right based on theories of social norms.

References

Abrams, D., & Levine, J. M. (2012). Norm formation: Revisiting Sherif's autokinetic illusion study. In J. R. Smith & S. A. Haslam (Eds.), *Social psychology: Revisiting the classic studies* (pp. 57–75). London: Sage Publications Ltd.

Arendt, H. (2006). *Eichmann in Jerusalem: A report on the banality of evil.* London: Penguin. (Original work published in 1963).

Asch, S. E. (1951). Effects of group pressure upon the modification and distortion of judgments. In H. Guetzkow (Ed.), *Groups, leadership and men; research in human relations* (pp. 177–190). Pittsburgh: Carnegie Press.
Asch, S. E. (1955). Opinions and social pressure. *Scientific American, 193* (5), 31–35.
Benjamin Jr, L. T., & Simpson, J. A. (2009). The power of the situation: The impact of Milgram's obedience studies on personality and social psychology. *American Psychologist, 64* (1), 12–19.
Bimber, B., & De Zúñiga, H. G. (2022). Social influence and political participation around the world. *European Political Science Review, 14* (2), 135–154.
Blais, A. (2000). *To vote or not to vote?: The merits and limits of rational choice theory.* Pittsburgh: University of Pittsburgh Press.
Blais, A., Galais, C., & Coulombe, M. (2019). The effect of social pressure from family and friends on turnout. *Journal of Social and Personal Relationships, 36* (9), 2824–2841.
Blass, T. (1991). Understanding behavior in the Milgram obedience experiment: The role of personality, situations, and their interactions. *Journal of Personality and Social Psychology, 60* (3), 398.
Blinder, S., Ford, R., & Ivarsflaten, E. (2013). The better angels of our nature: How the antiprejudice norm affects policy and party preferences in Great Britain and Germany. *American Journal of Political Science, 57* (4), 841–857.
Burger, J. M. (2009). Replicating Milgram: Would people still obey today? *American Psychologist, 64* (1), 1.
Bursztyn, L., Egorov, G., & Fiorin, S. (2020). From extreme to mainstream: The erosion of social norms. *American Economic Review, 110* (11), 3522–3548.
Cesarani, D. (2005). *Eichmann: His life and crimes.* London: Random House.
Costanzo, P. R. (1970). Conformity development as a function of self-blame. *Journal of Personality and Social Psychology, 14* (4), 366.
Coulombe, M., Blais, A., & Dassonneville, R. (2024). Do people vote to avoid disapproval? *Journal of Elections, Public Opinion and Parties,* (4), 727–739.
Crisp, R. J., Turner, R. N., & Meleady, R. (2024). *Essential social psychology.* London: SAGE Publications Limited.
Feldman, S., & Stenner, K. (1997). Perceived threat and authoritarianism. *Political Psychology, 18* (4), 741–770.
Franzen, A., & Mader, S. (2023). The power of social influence: A replication and extension of the Asch experiment. *Plos One, 18* (11), e0294325.
Gerber, A. S., Green, D. P., & Larimer, C. W. (2008). Social pressure and voter turnout: Evidence from a large-scale field experiment. *American Political Science Review, 102* (1), 33–48.
Green, D. P., & Gerber, A. S. (2019). *Get out the vote: How to increase voter turnout.* Washington, DC: Brookings Institution Press.
Haslam, S. A., & Reicher, S. (2007). Beyond the banality of evil: Three dynamics of an interactionist social psychology of tyranny. *Personality and Social Psychology Bulletin, 33* (5), 615–622.
Hogg, M. A. & Abrams, D. (1988). *Social identifications: A social psychology of intergroup relations and group processes.* New York: Routledge.
Kraus, M. W., Piff, P. K., Mendoza-Denton, R., Rheinschmidt, M. L., & Keltner, D. (2012). Social class, solipsism, and contextualism: How the rich are different from the poor. *Psychological Review, 119* (3), 546–572.

Marcus, G. E. (2013). *Political psychology: Neuroscience, genetics, and politics*. Oxford: Oxford University Press.

Milgram, S. (1963). Behavioral study of obedience. *The Journal of Abnormal and Social Psychology, 67*(4), 371–378.

Milgram, S. (1974). *Obedience to authority: An experimental view*. New York: Haper and Row.

Noelle-Neumann, E. (1974). The spiral of silence a theory of public opinion. *Journal of Communication, 24*(2), 43–51.

Noelle-Neumann, E. (1993). *The spiral of silence: Public opinion-our social skin*. Chicago: University of Chicago Press.

Sherif, M. (1936). *The psychology of social norms*. New York: Harper and Row.

Pronin, E., Berger, J., & Molouki, S. (2007). Alone in a crowd of sheep: Asymmetric perceptions of conformity and their roots in an introspection illusion. *Journal of Personality and Social Psychology, 92*(4), 585.

Takano, Y., & Sogon, S. (2008). Are Japanese more collectivistic than Americans? Examining conformity in in-groups and the reference-group effect. *Journal of Cross-Cultural Psychology, 39*(3), 237–250.

Valentim, V., Dinas, E., & Ziblatt, D. (2025). How mainstream politicians erode norms. *British Journal of Political Science, 55*, e105, 1–10.

Chapter 6

The Psychology of Intergroup Relations

Introduction

Social behavior can be distinguished between **interpersonal and intergroup behavior**. Interpersonal behavior between two or more individuals is the one that is "fully determined by their interpersonal relationships and individual characteristics, and not at all affected by various social groups or categories to which they respectively belong" (Tajfel & Turner, 1986, p. 34). A typical example of interpersonal behavior is the relationship between two childhood friends who may have different social backgrounds but, given the long history of their relationship, social background does not play any role in their interactions. On the other hand, intergroup behavior is determined by one's social group membership and unaffected by the individual relationships between those involved. To illustrate this, Tajfel gives the example of two opposing armies during a battle. Conduct here is determined by membership in one of the two armies. No matter what the individual characteristics of the opposing soldiers are, they do not play any role in the nature of the relationship. Intergroup relations involve perceiving who belongs to the ingroup and who does not, as well as the perceptions of ingroup and outgroup characteristics (Tajfel, 1970).

Interpersonal behavior: Interactions that occur between individuals, based on their personal characteristics and not influenced by group membership.

Intergroup behavior: Interactions that occur between individuals based on their group membership rather than personal characteristics.

Interpersonal and intergroup behaviors are rarely entirely distinct but rather represent a continuum, with most behaviors falling somewhere in between these two ends. In most social situations, interactions are determined both by social group membership and individual characteristics. Understanding when and why people may discriminate against outgroups or engage in intergroup conflict has been a focal point of social and political psychology since the birth

DOI: 10.4324/9781003460084-8

of these disciplines. In the rest of this chapter, I will provide an overview of major theoretical approaches to intergroup relations that focus on explaining and reducing prejudice and conflict.

Realistic Group Conflict Theory

Realistic Group Conflict Theory is one of the most influential theories in the social psychology of intergroup behavior. Developed by Muzafer Sherif in the 1950s and 1960s, it aims at understanding the conditions that contribute to intergroup hostility and intergroup cooperation. The basic thesis of this perspective is that intergroup hostility is evoked by competition and conflicting goals between social groups, and resolved by intergroup cooperation for the attainment of superordinate goals (Jackson, 1993; Sherif et al., 1988). Sherif and his colleagues tested the premises of the theory through a series of experiments. The most notable one was the Robbers Cave experiment (Sherif et al., 1988), which is today considered a classic study in social psychology (see Box 6.1).

Realistic Group Conflict Theory: A theory that explains intergroup hostility as emerging from competition over scarce resources or conflicting goals.

Box 6.1 The Robbers Cave Experiment

In the summer of 1954, Sherif and his colleagues studied the intergroup behavior of 24 eleven-year-old boys of middle-class Protestant families. The boys were divided into two groups designed to be as similar as possible in terms of character traits. They were then transferred separately by buses to the Robbers Cave State Park, a 200-acre area 150 miles south of Oklahoma City. The boys were never informed that they were taking part in a research experiment, while Sherif and colleagues posed as camp personnel.

The experiment unfolded in three separate stages, each lasting approximately one week. Phase 1 was the *ingroup formation* phase. During this stage, the two groups were in different parts of the park and unaware of each other's presence. The boys in each group were encouraged through group activities to collaborate with the aim of pursuing common goals. They assumed different roles within their respective groups, with some boys taking leadership roles and others being more reserved. During this stage, the groups developed norms and decided on their group names ("Eagles" and "Rattlers") as well as other symbols of group identification, such as songs. Phase 2 was the *intergroup tension* phase. Having established the two ingroups, the researchers aimed at creating friction under controlled conditions. The two groups "found themselves in competition for given goals and in conditions implying some frustration in relation to one another" (Sherif et al., 1988, p. 24). They first informed them that there was another group in the camp and subsequently they organized competitive activities in the form of tournaments (e.g., baseball or tug-of-war) that used cumulative scoring, and members of the winning team received rewards. The tournaments had behavioral consequences: the groups gradually started exhibiting high ingroup solidarity and negative attitudes toward the outgroup (i.e., the other group of boys), expressed through derogation and name-calling. The aggression toward the outgroup escalated with each day and the researchers had to intervene to physically separate the boys before becoming directly violent. Moreover, Sherif and his colleagues observed that negative attitudes toward the outgroup persisted even after the competitive events had ended.

Phase 3 was the *integration phase*, where the researchers aimed at testing different interventions focused on reducing the group tension. The researchers first established that – in line with their expectations – increasing contact between the groups in the context of positive activities (e.g., watching a film together) did little to appease the tension between the groups. To this end, Sherif and colleagues introduced *superordinate goals*, or in other words, goals that could only be attained through collaboration. For instance, one such activity concerned a collective tug-of-war to release a truck that carried the camp food from mud (and, unknowingly to the participants, had been staged there by the researchers). Under these conditions the boys tended to cooperate across group lines to resolve the situation. This, in turn, fostered a sense of interdependence between the two groups, which led to a notable decrease in hostility and aggression.

Realistic Group Conflict Theory considers intergroup conflict as arising from real or perceived competition over scarce material or symbolic resources. Intergroup competition, where gains by one group result in loss for another, strengthens the identification with the ingroup and increases negative attitudes, stereotyping, and hostility toward the outgroup. The perception of competition with outgroups is transmitted to members of the ingroup through the family, school, media, and other socialization processes. In Sherif's words, "an individual's prejudices are acquired as he becomes a member of his group" (1948, p. 66). The socialization aspect makes intergroup hostility enduring and difficult to change through direct contact with an outgroup (Sherif, 1948). In other words, even if a member of the group does not personally feel in competition with outgroups, they may still display hostility toward an outgroup based on other ingroup members' competition with the same outgroup. On the other hand, collaboration in pursuing superordinate goals resolves conflict by lowering aggression and fostering a sense of interdependence. However, these collaborative efforts need to be persistent for friction to be reduced.

Sherif's studies were ground-breaking as they investigated systematically for the first time group formation, hostility, and cooperation. There is much subsequent research that supports the premises of Realistic Group Conflict Theory. For example, studies have found that opposition to immigration among natives intensifies when there is (perceived) conflict over scarce resources. People with highly specific occupational skills and limited options for changing jobs are more likely to be hostile toward immigration because they perceive immigrants as potential competitors for their own jobs (Pardos-Prado & Xena, 2019). Similarly, anti-immigration sentiment runs high during periods of economic stagnation when resource competition between natives and immigrants is higher (Dancygier & Donnelly, 2014). These findings are in line with the main hypothesis of Realistic Group Conflict Theory: intergroup conflict arises because of competition for resources between social groups.

The Minimal Group Paradigm

In the late 1960s, Tajfel and his colleagues, inspired by Sherif's findings, became interested in further exploring the reasons behind the emergence of intergroup conflict. The questions that motivated their research were fundamental. First, is intergroup conflict always rooted in group competition over resources? Second, if competition is not always a necessary condition, which other factors predict whether groups will find themselves in conflict? Their initial idea was to design experiments that placed participants in a group situation, but where the major known causes of conflict (e.g., competition) were eliminated. In this way the researchers could discover the ***minimal*** conditions necessary for the development of intergroup hostility by gradually introducing elements until conflict was achieved. This method of elimination is often referred to as **The Minimal Group Paradigm**.

Minimal Group Paradigm: An experimental method developed by Henri Tajfel aiming at understanding the minimum conditions required for intergroup discrimination.

In the experiments, participants believed they were allocated to different groups based on some superficial criteria (in reality, the allocation was random). In some variations, respondents believed they were allocated to groups according to their estimations on the number of dots in a screen ("overestimators" versus "underestimators", Tajfel et al., 1971); in another variation, allocation was based on their preference for the paintings of Wassily Kandinsky versus Paul Klee (Tajfel, 1970). Importantly, the groups were always defined based on flimsy criteria: participants were unaware of the identities of other members and at no stage did they interact with them. Moreover, the groups existed solely for the specific task, with no history or future beyond it. After the formation of the groups, Tajfel and colleagues asked participants to allocate points (which sometimes had real but small monetary value) to members of their own group and to members of the other group. Participants would not personally benefit in either way and their choices would not become known to anyone other than the researchers.

Under these conditions, the task seemed absurd (Hornsey, 2008). How is one supposed to allocate rewards to people without any background information other than a preference for Klee over Kandinsky? The best guess is that they would try to allocate points equally between groups or at random, as the task was effectively meaningless due to the superficiality of the group formation. This was in fact what the researchers themselves expected (Hornsey, 2008). What they found, instead, was startling. Participants tended to systematically favor their ingroup – no matter how arbitrarily defined – and discriminate against the outgroup, even at the cost of smaller rewards for their own group.

Through these experiments, Tajfel and colleagues realized that the minimal conditions for intergroup discrimination to manifest were much more minimal than Realistic Group Conflict Theory would anticipate (1970; Billig & Tajfel, 1973). Not only competition or resource scarcity was not a necessary condition for the development of outgroup discrimination, but prejudicial behavior also took place in the absence of self-interest and any history of contact between the groups. Put differently, intergroup discrimination seemed to arise by the mere awareness of belonging to a distinct group. In fact, in some variations of the experiment, the researchers explicitly told participants they were entirely randomly assigned into two groups, only to find that ingroup bias still occurred (Billig & Tajfel, 1973). It seemed that people have a natural tendency to favor their ingroup, no matter how superficial the ingroup is.

Social Identity Theory

The unexpected findings from the Minimal Group Paradigm experiments inspired Tajfel to develop **Social Identity Theory** in collaboration with his graduate student John Turner (e.g., Tajfel, 1978; Tajfel & Turner, 1986). The theory offers an elaborate theoretical account of both the psychological functions of group membership and the mechanisms underlying intergroup

Social Identity Theory: A theory positing that individuals derive a part of their self-esteem from the groups they belong to, which may lead to ingroup favoritism and may foster outgroup discrimination.

discrimination. The starting point of Social Identity Theory is the premise that people cope with the complexity of the social world around them by organizing it in terms of social groups. This process is referred to as social categorization. Groups here refer to purely cognitive entities, that is, they are not necessarily based on any "real" characteristics. Social categorization helps people save cognitive effort, which is important when trying to make sense of a complex social environment.

Social Identity Theory posits that people are psychologically motivated to hold positive social identities. This is because belonging to groups of high status or with desirable qualities increases people's self-esteem and contributes to a positive self-image. In simple terms, being a member of a high-status social group makes us feel good about ourselves. To achieve a positive image (for the self and the ingroup), we tend to compare our group with relevant outgroups seeking positive distinctiveness. As Turner puts it, "to achieve positive social identity, ingroup-outgroup comparisons must yield perceived differences which favour the ingroup" (1978, p. 235). Ingroup favoritism, in turn motivates outgroup derogation. This does not necessarily imply hostility toward outsiders. Hostility arises when ingroup favoritism is combined with intergroup competition or perceived outgroup threat (Brewer, 1999). Social comparisons foster ingroup bias and strengthen identification with the ingroup, particularly when people find themselves in situations where social categories become salient. This is expressed through an adherence to ingroup norms and self-stereotyping in line with the qualities of the ingroup and at the expense of personal independence.

In summary, social identification involves three steps. Social categorization, which refers to the formation of "us" versus "them" perceptions based on perceived differences between groups; second, social identification, or the sense of belonging to a group; and third, comparison with the outgroup, which strengthens ingroup bias (favoring the ingroup as opposed to the outgroup) and outgroup derogation, potentially leading to outgroup hostility. Social identity theorists claim that this framework can help us understand the increased allocations to the ingroup compared to the outgroup in the Minimal Group Paradigm experiments. Offering increased rewards to members of one's own group can be explained by ingroup bias, outgroup discrimination, and a motivation to affirm the high status of the ingroup.

However, ascertaining positive distinctiveness through social comparison has its limits. In cases where membership in a given group does not contribute to a positive social identity, the individual may try to leave and join a higher status group that will contribute to positive self-esteem (Tajfel, 1978). However, sometimes leaving a group is impossible. For instance, it would be hard for someone to change their racial or ethnic background. In other cases, leaving a group may clash with important values and beliefs, for example, in the case of religion. According to Social Identity Theory, in these situations, there are two possible strategies. One is to change one's attitude toward the ingroup by, for example, reinterpreting its supposedly unwelcome qualities in a positive way. For instance, the Queer movement in the 1990s reinterpreted a stigmatizing label in a positive and empowering manner, so that "where before it referred to despised distinctiveness, it now refers to celebrated distinctiveness" (Galinsky et al., 2003, p. 231). Another strategy is to engage in social action that would lead to improvements in the group's status. Such examples include the LGBTQI, Civil Rights, or Black Lives Matter movements.

Political psychologists have drawn on Social Identity Theory to investigate a wealth of political outcomes, including social movements, political participation, or partisanship (Huddy et al., 2015; Mason, 2018). For example, Social Identity Theory helps us understand the increasing hostility across partisan lines, which is observed in many democracies (e.g., Bergman & Fernández, 2024; Wagner, 2024). In her seminal study on the origins of partisan animosity in the United States, Mason employs Social Identity Theory to argue that contemporary partisan identities are solidifying because people with specific social characteristics (e.g., place of residence, education level, or type of community) increasingly align themselves with specific political parties (Mason, 2018).

Stereotypes

Stereotypes refer to "socially shared sets of beliefs about traits that are characteristic of members of a social category" (Greenwald & Banaji, 1995, p. 14). Stereotypical perceptions of a social group shape our behavior toward individual members of this group. In other words, stereotypes constitute the cognitive basis of discrimination. A broad stream of research has shown that stereotypes lead to prejudice. For example, studies have found that employers, motivated to recruit productive and competent workers, often rely on stereotyping in hiring decisions, which result in discrimination against women and ethnic minorities (e.g., Ndobo et al., 2018). In the housing market, real estate agents often rely on stereotypes to choose desirable tenants (e.g., Korver-Glenn, 2018). In elections, voters employ stereotypes around gender or ethnic background to assess a politician's competence as well as their positions on issues (McDermott, 1998; Schneider & Bos, 2019).

Stereotypes: Socially shared sets of beliefs about the typical traits and behaviors of members of a given social group.

The sources of stereotypes go beyond our direct experiences with members of social groups. They are transmitted through socialization and our social environment. The mass media play a key role in this process. News stories, films, novels, series, and video games often transmit and reinforce all sorts of stereotypes about gender, race, ethnicity, nationality, religion, sexual orientation, occupation, physical attractiveness, residence, immigration status, preferred music style, and several other social characteristics (e.g., Bazzini et al., 2010; Burgess et al., 2011; Xu et al., 2019). Social psychologists have long discovered that not only do most people agree on the stereotypical characteristics of different social groups (e.g., Katz & Braly, 1933), but also that children as young as six years old are aware of and internalize them (Cvencek et al., 2011). Characteristics such as gender or race are so strongly embedded that our brains automatically react to individuals from these categories without us realizing it. Hence, stereotyping may take place even outside of our conscious awareness (i.e., implicit attitudes, see Greenwald & Banaji, 1995).

When we discuss stereotypes in everyday conversations, most of the time we refer to the negative stereotyping of low-status groups. People who draw on stereotypes are often perceived as shallow, unintelligent, or even bigoted. However, stereotypes are far more nuanced than we tend to assume in daily life. For instance, stereotypes may well involve positive generalizations about a social group (e.g., scientists, firefighters) or they may simultaneously combine positive and negative qualities. For instance, cheerleaders "simultaneously include the traits of being physically attractive (positive) and unintelligent (negative)" (Greenwald & Banaji, 1995, p. 14). Moreover, it has been repeatedly shown that people can also adopt and internalize negative stereotypes about their own group (negative self-stereotyping).

Why Do People Use Stereotypes?

Why are we so inclined to use stereotypes? What are the psychological functions that they serve? Social psychologists began exploring these questions as early as the beginning of the 20th century. In his now classic book *Public Opinion* (1922), Walter Lippmann argued that relying on stereotypes is an inevitable part of human thought and reasoning. He suggested that stereotypes offer an immensely helpful tool for navigating a complex social world. According to Lippmann, there are sufficient uniformities among groups that allow for generalizations, which are necessary for the organization and simplification of our social environment. Hence, stereotypes fulfill a cognitive function by making the world more manageable and predictable, thereby helping us process information. Without stereotypes our brains would struggle with chaos as we would have to treat any person we come across as entirely unique without any shared characteristics with anyone else (Glynn et al., 2004). In Lippmann's words, "The attempt to see all things freshly and in detail, rather than as types and generalities, is exhausting, and among busy affairs it is practically out of the question" (1922, p. 88). Our brains build taxonomies based on similarities: university professors, the working class, Trump voters, librarians, vegans, politicians, or Taylor Swift fans all exist as abstract categories in our minds helping us to mentally organize our social environment. Lippmann acknowledges that stereotypes are often inaccurate and misleading, making us "liable to serious confusion" (1922, p. 93). Nonetheless, according to the cognitive function perspective, stereotypes are necessary for dealing with a complex world.

In addition to cognitive functions, stereotypes also fulfill core intergroup functions. According to the **Stereotype Content Model (SCM)** developed by social psychologist Susan Fiske and her colleagues, when people meet others they want to know (a) their intent (positive or negative) and (b) capability (Fiske et al., 2002, p. 879). These correspond to two key dimensions that are fundamental in stereotype formation (Fiske et al., 2002). The first dimension captures *warmth*, or the extent to which a member of a social group is perceived as "warm, trustworthy, friendly, honest, likable, and sincere" – or not (Fiske, 2018, p. 68). The second is *competence*, which captures characteristics such as intelligence, efficiency, confidence, and assertiveness – or their absence (Fiske, 2018; Fiske et al., 2002). Based on these dimensions, Fiske and colleagues distinguish between four types of groups:

> **Stereotype Content Model (SCM):** A theoretical model arguing that stereotypes include two core dimensions: warmth and competence.

1 Groups that are stereotyped as high in warmth and competence (e.g., religious leaders or the middle class) tend to be highly regarded and admired.
2 Groups perceived as both untrustworthy and incompetent (e.g., drug addicts) face contempt and disgust.
3 Groups that are seen as warm but not competent (e.g., disabled people) tend to receive sympathy.
4 Groups that are perceived as highly competent but lacking warmth (e.g., the rich) simultaneously receive admiration and resentment.

Yet, what conditions lead people to perceive some groups as competent, others as warm, and others as neither? Early psychological theory argued that stereotypes are employed to justify and advance our social position. In other words, they represent "the defense of our position in society" (Lippmann, 1922, p. 95), contributing to our self-esteem and the advancement of our economic and social interests (e.g., Katz & Braly, 1933; Lippmann, 1922). A classic example is that stereotyping the poor as lazy (and therefore undeserving of help) is more common among people with higher socioeconomic status. This suggests that a stereotype can be used to justify one's social status vis-à-vis others. Jost and Banaji call this ego-justification (1994). Similarly, Gordon Allport, a leading psychologist working on prejudice, argued that the main function of stereotypes is to justify our conduct in relation to the stereotyped outgroup (Allport, 1979). For instance, a police officer may justify excessive use of force against an immigrant coming from a country stereotyped for violent crime. As Jost and Banaji argue, however, people employ stereotypes even about groups they have never been in contact with. Further, if we only employed stereotypes to justify our social status or conduct toward others, we would expect disadvantaged groups to hold different stereotypes toward other discriminated outgroups than those held by advantaged groups (Jost & Banaji, 1994). Yet, as mentioned earlier, there is broad agreement about the stereotypical characteristics of different social groups, regardless of the stereotype holder's relationship to them.

Social Identity Theory can help us understand why stereotypes may develop even in the absence of any personal relationship through the motivation to maintain a positive social identity against outgroups. According to Jost and Banaji, stereotypes may not only be formed based on the advancement of our individual interests, but also of the interests of our social group. Hence, we do not need to have any direct relation with a member of a stereotyped group if some of our ingroup members do. Indeed, the need for positive differentiation compared to outgroups could explain why two disadvantaged groups may hold negative stereotypes about each other. Still, it is hard to explain why members of stigmatized groups engage in negative self-stereotyping (Jost & Banaji, 1994).

Inspired by this puzzle about negative self-stereotyping, Jost and Banaji developed **System Justification Theory** (1994; See also Jost, 2019; Jost et al., 2004). Gradually, the theory expanded well beyond the psychological motivations underlying negative self-stereotyping, providing a broad and rich theoretical account on how intergroup inequality is preserved and justified. The theory argues that some individuals are not only motivated to defend their individual and group interests, but they are also motivated to justify the social and economic system as a whole. This is because viewing the status quo as just, fair, and legitimate decreases negative emotionality and increases life satisfaction. In their preference to perceive the world as fair and predictable, some individuals are willing to rationalize and justify existing social arrangements, even if they are unfair or harmful. Importantly, this system-justifying tendency exists even among those who are disadvantaged by existing social arrangements. As Jost and Banaji argue, "the justification

System justification: The tendency to perceive and endorse the existing social, economic, and political systems as fair, legitimate, and desirable – even when these systems create or reinforce inequalities.

Table 6.1 The Three Motivational Functions of Stereotypes (Jost & Banaji, 1994)

	Function	*Example*
Ego-justification	Justify one's social position or conduct vis-à-vis others	A person from a higher socioeconomic background may stereotype the poor as lazy and deserving of their fate to justify wealth inequality
Group justification	Justify one's group position or group conduct vis-à-vis other social groups	Negative stereotyping of groups that one has no personal contact with, for example, Russians by Americans and vice versa during the Cold War
System justification	Justify the social and economic system that one is a member of	A person from a low social status group may negatively stereotype their own group as lazy or undeserving, motivated by the need to justify existing social hierarchies

of the status quo frequently appears to outweigh the individual's defense of group interests" (1994, p. 9). Hence, stereotypes are developed not only to defend individual or group interests but also to defend the societal and economic system in general. Hence, low-status groups may endorse negative stereotypes about their own groups motivated by their need to justify the existing social and economic systems on which they depend. In other words, "the powerful are stereotyped even by the powerless, in such a way that their success is explained or justified; meanwhile the powerless are stereotyped (and self-stereotyped) in a way that their plight is well-deserved and similarly justified" (1994, p. 304) (Table 6.1).

Intergroup Contact Theory

So far, we have predominantly focused on how intergroup conflict and discrimination emerge and manifest. Yet, research has also identified conditions that may lead to the reduction of prejudice. A prominent example is **Intergroup Contact Theory**. This theory argues that under certain conditions, contact between members of different social groups can reduce prejudice and foster positive intergroup relationships (Allport, 1979; Williams, 1947). Allport (1979) proposed a number of optimal conditions for contact to reduce intergroup bias. These were: equal status between majority and minority groups, cooperation among group members, the pursuit of common goals, and an environment that supports contact either formally (e.g., the military

Intergroup Contact Theory: A theory proposing that, under specific conditions, interpersonal contact between members of different social groups can reduce prejudice and improve intergroup relations.

or a school or a workplace) or informally, through social norms and community attitudes (e.g., neighborhood activities). According to Pettigrew (1998), contact under these conditions provides new information about the outgroup that may contradict and counteract negative stereotypical perceptions. Further, and critically, positive contact between group members enhances attitudes toward outgroups by decreasing negative emotions, such as intergroup anxiety (the anxiety we feel when interacting with people who are different from us) and increasing positive emotions, such as empathy toward outgroup members. Another process by which contact fosters attitude change is through a reevaluation of the ingroup following the realization that "ingroup norms and customs turn out not to be the only ways to manage the social world" (i.e., deprovincialization, Pettigrew, 1998, p. 72). Subsequent research argues that positive intergroup contact is enough to attenuate prejudice, even in the absence of Allport's conditions (Pettigrew & Tropp, 2006).

Intergroup contact theory has inspired a very large wave of research that mostly supports its key premises. Pettigrew and Tropp synthesized the findings of a large number of studies testing the contact hypothesis proposed by Allport (1979) and found that 94 per cent of the samples "show an inverse relationship between intergroup contact and prejudice" (2006, p. 757). For instance, studies have found that contact with outgroup members leads to positive intergroup relations in neighborhoods (Schmid et al., 2014), the workplace (Di Bernardo et al., 2022), and university dormitories (Shook & Fazio, 2008). Contact has also been found to have lasting effects on political behavior. For instance, White Americans who had an African American next-door neighbor during childhood were more likely to vote Democrat seven decades later (Brown et al., 2021). Notably, research has shown that in addition to face-to-face contact, mediated contact with outgroups, through celebrities or fictional characters, can also tackle prejudice: Ala Alrababah et al. (2021) illustrated that the success of the star football player for Liverpool F.C. and devout Muslim, Mohamed Salah, led to a significant reduction in Islamophobia among the club's fans. Another study found that mediated contact in the form of watching material by transgender creators on TikTok decreased transphobia among cisgendered individuals (Jolley et al., 2025).

Importantly, studies show that when contact with people from distinct groups is limited or absent, the sudden appearance of outgroups in the social environment may increase prejudice. For example, in a cleverly designed experiment, Enos hired two Spanish-speaking men to stand and discuss between them on a train platform during commuting hours at Boston's predominantly White suburbs. His goal was to "make people think that their neighborhood was experiencing demographic change due to immigration" (2017, p. 108). By comparing the attitudes of the commuters waiting on the platform with the Spanish-speaking men to commuters who had not been exposed to the intervention, Enos found that the mere presence of the Spanish-speaking young men for three days was enough to boost hostility toward immigration among commuters who were exposed to the intervention. However, after ten days, when the Spanish-speaking duo became more familiar to the commuters and small interactions started taking place, hostility waned. In one of the Spanish-speaking men's words, "people have started to recognize and smile to us" (2017, p. 125). Another study conducted in the Greek islands near Turkey, which function as reception spots for many Middle Eastern, Asian, and African refugees, found that the presence of refugees – typically confined to isolated camps and disconnected from local communities – led to increased hostility among native residents (Hangartner et al., 2019). These findings reinforce the notion that the mere presence of outgroups is not always enough to reduce prejudice, and in some cases it may even intensify it. Instead, intergroup contact needs to take place under favorable conditions and needs to be experienced as positive.

Conclusion

The relationships between social groups have been a focal point of social and political psychology for decades. This chapter presented an overview of theory and research in intergroup relations. Realistic Group Conflict Theory argues that competition over resources is the main driver of intergroup conflict, while Social Identity Theory posits that intergroup conflict arises by comparing ingroup and outgroup traits and looking for positive distinctiveness. We also explored the cognitive functions and content of stereotypes, as well as the ways in which positive contact can tackle biased thinking and reduce intergroup prejudice. A common point across these different theoretical perspectives is that they explain prejudice and conflict focusing on the social context, rather than on individual characteristics. This does not mean that individual predispositions do not play a role. For instance, Allport acknowledges that not all individuals are equally prone to informing their preferences through contact with outgroups. Research has also shown that individual psychological characteristics, such as authoritarianism (see Chapter 2) or personality traits (see Chapter 3), condition whether contact with outgroups will lead to a reduction of prejudice or an increase in hostility (e.g., Johnston et al., 2015).

Further Reading

Allport, G. W. (1979). *The nature of prejudice* (25th Anniversary Edition). New York: Perseus. The seminal study of Allport on the psychology of prejudice and intergroup relations. (Original work published 1954).

Jost, J. T. (2020). *A theory of system justification*. Cambridge, MA: Harvard University Press. A comprehensive account of system justification theory and its applications.

References

Allport, G. W. (1979). *The nature of prejudice* (25th Anniversary Edition). New York: Perseus. (Original work published 1954).

Alrababah, A., Marble, W., Mousa, S., & Siegel, A. (2021). Can exposure to celebrities reduce prejudice? The effect of Mohamed Salah on Islamophobic behaviors and attitudes. *American Political Science Review, 115* (4), 1111–1128.

Bazzini, D., Curtin, L., Joslin, S., Regan, S., & Martz, D. (2010). Do animated Disney characters portray and promote the beauty–goodness stereotype? *Journal of Applied Social Psychology, 40* (10), 2687–2709.

Bergman, M., & Fernández, P. (2024). Affective polarization in Latin America: A research note. *Latin American Politics and Society, 67*, 114–132.

Billig, M., & Tajfel, H. (1973). Social categorization and similarity in intergroup behaviour. *European Journal of Social Psychology, 3* (1), 27–52.

Brewer, M. B. (1999). The psychology of prejudice: Ingroup love and outgroup hate? *Journal of Social Issues, 55* (3), 429–444.

Brown, J. R., Enos, R. D., Feigenbaum, J., & Mazumder, S. (2021). Childhood cross-ethnic exposure predicts political behavior seven decades later: Evidence from linked administrative data. *Science Advances, 7* (24), eabe8432.

Burgess, M. C., Dill, K. E., Stermer, S. P., Burgess, S. R., & Brown, B. P. (2011). Playing with prejudice: The prevalence and consequences of racial stereotypes in video games. *Media Psychology, 14* (3), 289–311.

Cvencek, D., Meltzoff, A. N., & Greenwald, A. G. (2011). Math–gender stereotypes in elementary school children. *Child Development, 82* (3), 766–779.

Dancygier, R., & Donnelly, M. (2014). Attitudes toward immigration in good times and bad. In N. Bermeo & L. M. Bartels (Eds.), *Mass politics in tough times: Opinions, votes, and protest in the great recession* (pp. 148–184). Oxford: Oxford University Press.

Di Bernardo, G. A., Vezzali, L., Birtel, M. D., Stathi, S., Ferrari, B., Giovannini, D., & Pettigrew, T. F. (2022). The role of optimal conditions and intergroup contact in promoting positive intergroup relations in and out of the workplace: A study with ethnic majority and minority workers. *Group Processes & Intergroup Relations, 25* (6), 1516–1533.

Enos, R. D. (2017). *The space between us: Social geography and politics*. Cambridge: Cambridge University Press.

Fiske, S. T. (2018). Stereotype content: Warmth and competence endure. *Current Directions in Psychological Science, 27* (2), 67–73.

Fiske, S. T., Cuddy, A. J., Glick, P., & Xu, J. (2002). A model of (often mixed) stereotype content: Competence and warmth respectively follow from perceived status and competition. *Journal of Personality and Social Psychology, 82* (6), 878–902.

Galinsky, A. D., Hugenberg, K., Groom, C., & Bodenhausen, G. V. 2003. The reappropriation of stigmatizing labels: Implications for social identity. In J. Polzer (ed.), *Identity issues in groups* (pp. 221–256). Leeds: Emerald Group Publishing Limited.

Glynn, C. J., Herbst, S., O'Keefe, G. J., Shapiro, R. Y., & Lindeman, M. (2004). *Public opinion* (2nd ed.). Oxford: Westview Press.

Greenwald, A. G., & Banaji, M. R. (1995). Implicit social cognition: Attitudes, self-esteem, and stereotypes. *Psychological Review*, *102* (1), 4.

Hangartner, D., Dinas, E., Marbach, M., Matakos, K., & Xefteris, D. (2019). Does exposure to the refugee crisis make natives more hostile? *American Political Science Review*, *113* (2), 442–455.

Hornsey, M. J. (2008). Social identity theory and self-categorization theory: A historical review. *Social and Personality Psychology Compass*, *2* (1), 204–222.

Huddy, L., Mason, L., & Aarøe, L. (2015). Expressive partisanship: Campaign involvement, political emotion, and partisan identity. *American Political Science Review*, *109* (1), 1–17.

Jackson, J. W. (1993). Realistic group conflict theory: A review and evaluation of the theoretical and empirical literature. *The Psychological Record*, *43* (3), 395–413.

Johnston, C. D., Newman, B. J., & Velez, Y. (2015). Ethnic change, personality, and polarization over immigration in the American public. *Public Opinion Quarterly*, *79* (3), 662–686.

Jolley, D., Paterson, J. L., Deric, D., Lovato, T., & McCarthy, J. (2025). Exploring how parasocial intergroup contact with transgender influencers on TikTok reduces transgender conspiracy beliefs. *Journal of Community & Applied Social Psychology*, *35* (1), e70020.

Jost, J. T. (2019). A quarter century of system justification theory: Questions, answers, criticisms, and societal applications. *British Journal of Social Psychology*, *58* (2), 263–314.

Jost, J. T., & Banaji, M. R. (1994). The role of stereotyping in system-justification and the production of false consciousness. *British Journal of Social Psychology*, *33* (1), 1–27.

Jost, J. T., Banaji, M. R., & Nosek, B. A. (2004). A decade of system justification theory: Accumulated evidence of conscious and unconscious bolstering of the status quo. *Political Psychology*, *25* (6), 881–919.

Katz, D., & Braly, K. (1933). Racial stereotypes of one hundred college students. *The Journal of Abnormal and Social Psychology*, *28* (3), 280.

Korver-Glenn, E. (2018). Compounding inequalities: How racial stereotypes and discrimination accumulate across the stages of housing exchange. *American Sociological Review*, *83* (4), 627–656.

Lippmann, W. (1922). *Public opinion*. New York: Harcourt Brace.

Mason, L. (2018). *Uncivil agreement: How politics became our identity*. Chicago: University of Chicago Press.

McDermott, M. L. (1998). Race and gender cues in low-information elections. *Political Research Quarterly*, *51* (4), 895–918.

Ndobo, A., Faure, A., Boisselier, J., & Giannaki, S. (2018). The ethno-racial segmentation jobs: The impacts of the occupational stereotypes on hiring decisions. *The Journal of Social Psychology*, *158* (6), 663–679.

Pardos-Prado, S., & Xena, C. (2019). Skill specificity and attitudes toward immigration. *American Journal of Political Science*, *63* (2), 286–304.

Pettigrew, T. F. (1998). Intergroup contact theory. *Annual Review of Psychology*, *49* (1), 65–85.

Pettigrew, T. F., & Tropp, L. R. (2006). A meta-analytic test of intergroup contact theory. *Journal of Personality and Social Psychology*, *90* (5), 751.

Schmid, K., Ramiah, A. A., & Hewstone, M. (2014). Neighborhood ethnic diversity and trust: The role of intergroup contact and perceived threat. *Psychological Science*, *25* (3), 665–674.

Schneider, M. C., & Bos, A. L. (2019). The application of social role theory to the study of gender in politics. *Political Psychology, 40*, 173–213.

Sherif, M. (1948). The necessity of considering current issues as part and parcel of persistent major problems, illustrated by the problem of prejudice. *International Journal of Opinion & Attitude Research*, (2), 63–68.

Sherif, M., Harvey, O., & White, B. (1988). *The robbers cave experiment: Intergroup conflict and cooperation.* Middletown, CT: Wesleyan University Press. (Original work published 1961).

Shook, N. J., & Fazio, R. H. (2008). Interracial roommate relationships: An experimental field test of the contact hypothesis. *Psychological Science, 19*(7), 717–723.

Tajfel, H. (1970). Experiments in intergroup discrimination. *Scientific American, 223*(5), 96–103.

Tajfel, H. (1978). Social categorization, social identity and social comparison. In H. Tajfel (Ed.), *Differentiation between social groups: Studies in the social psychology of intergroup relations* (pp. 61–76). London: Academic Press.

Tajfel, H., Billig, M. G., Bundy, R. P., & Flament, C. (1971). Social categorization and intergroup behaviour. *European Journal of Social Psychology, 1*(2), 149–178.

Tajfel, H., & Turner, J. C. (1986). The social identity theory of intergroup behavior. In S. Worchel & W. G. Austin (Eds.), *Psychology of intergroup relations* (pp. 7–24). Chicago: Nelson-Hall.

Turner, J. C. (1978). Social comparison, similarity, and ingroup favoritism. In H. Tajfel (Ed.), *Differentiation between social groups: Studies in the social psychology of intergroup relations* (pp. 235–250). London: Academic Press.

Wagner, M. (2024). Affective polarization in Europe. *European Political Science Review, 16*(3), 378–392.

Williams Jr, R. M. (1947). *The reduction of intergroup tensions: A survey of research on problems of ethnic, racial, and religious group relations.* New York: Social Science Research Council.

Xu, H., Zhang, Z., Wu, L., & Wang, C. J. (2019). The Cinderella Complex: Word embeddings reveal gender stereotypes in movies and books. *PloS One, 14* (11), e0225385.

Chapter 7

Political Information Processing

Introduction

The political world is highly complex. Politicians, journalists, and other public figures engage in debates over political issues whose historical context, proposed solutions, and potential impacts are often difficult to decipher. Would the introduction of a wealth tax reduce economic inequality? What effects would the nationalization of railway or energy companies have for consumers? How effective are sanctions against authoritarian regimes? How does membership in international organizations impact domestic policies? These are examples of questions that many citizens find challenging – and for good reason.

Nevertheless, a requirement of good citizenship is following political affairs and holding informed opinions on the important issues of the day. On election day, citizens are expected to carefully consider party proposals over how to best address these issues and cast their votes in line with their own interests, values, and political beliefs. Such a process requires extensive knowledge about current affairs. Is it realistic to expect citizens to be this well informed? And, crucially, if citizens lack the political knowledge required for holding informed opinions, how do they reach political decisions on complex political issues? These are central questions in political psychology and have generated a long debate over what people know about politics and whether and how meaningful political decisions can be reached in the absence of extensive political information.

Political Information among Mass Publics

Even before the era of mass polling and quantitative surveys, scholars were suspicious that average citizens had little knowledge about politics (e.g., Lippmann, 1922). Part of this suspicion was based on the concept of **rational ignorance** (e.g., Downs, 1957). Why is it rational to be ignorant over political affairs? According to Anthony Downs, an economist who wrote extensively on rationality and politics, the primary goal of the acquisition of political information is to cast an informed vote that best represents an individual's interests.

DOI: 10.4324/9781003460084-9

However, in mass elections a single individual's vote will never decide the electoral result. This means that political information is a bad investment for most citizens: It comes with high costs in terms of time to follow political news and effort to understand which candidate is closer to one's interests. Yet, from an individual's perspective, the returns of this investment in time and effort are essentially zero because one single vote will never decide the electoral outcome. Hence, according to this perspective, political information is not of much use to everyday citizens, unless they follow politics for pleasure or for reasons of social status.

Despite the long-term suspicion that mass political knowledge is low, the findings of the first systematic opinion surveys in the United States in the 1950s and 1960s that directly addressed this question came as a shock to many scholars and pundits. One of the key discoveries of these pioneer studies was that most voters did not think of politics in ideological terms and that around four out of ten were entirely unaware of what "liberalism" or "conservatism" meant (Campbell et al., 1960; Converse, 1964). In a landmark study in political behavior, Philip Converse showed that the average citizen lacked a coherent and organized set of political attitudes (1964). For example, one's attitudes toward welfare policies were unrelated to their preferences over taxation, even though the two are clearly related. He also found that political attitudes were highly unstable over time, with many citizens changing sides on key issues in a short time span for no apparent reason. Based on these observations he estimated that a considerable portion of the American public lacked meaningful political attitudes and seemed to respond to public opinion surveys at random. His conclusion hit a very pessimistic tone: "large portions of an electorate do not have meaningful beliefs even on issues that have formed the basis for intense political controversy among elites for substantial periods of time" (Converse, 1964, p. 245).

These findings painted a very grim picture of mass electorates, casting doubt on one of the pillars of representative democracy: the ability of citizens to provide elites with meaningful preferences that policymakers can transform into policies. From a politician's perspective, what is the value of trying to follow public opinion when so many citizens do not seem to hold meaningful political preferences?

Some researchers argued that the fact that broad publics may possess little political sophistication is not necessarily detrimental to an effective democracy. In their book *The Rational Public* (1992) Page and Shapiro investigated a large series of polling data across several years finding that, as a whole, the public's preferences are both relatively stable over time and meaningful – in the sense that they change in line with important events. But how is it possible that citizen opinions are both random and meaningful? The answer, according to the authors, lies in the unit of measurement. If instead of looking at opinions at the individual level one examines whether and how public opinion changes *as a whole* they would certainly not get the image that a significant portion of the public decides at random. Instead they would conclude that the public generally has stable policy preferences that are updated in the light of key social and political developments. This is possible because aggregating a large set of individual responses cancels out random opinions. In other words when there is a large number of people each individual preference that is made at random will be canceled out by another opposite preference that has also been made at random. What remains is the minority of the public that follows politics close enough to react to events and provide elites with meaningful policy inputs. Consequently, according to Page and Shapiro, even if the majority of the electorate decides at random, public opinion as a whole can still be meaningful and coherent, agreeing, for example, with increased defense spending in the aftermath of an international diplomatic crisis.

The idea that the public as a collective provides informed inputs to political elites even if the majority decides at random has been met with skepticism by some scholars. For instance, an assumption of the theory is the full randomness of individual policy choices. This however may not be satisfied in practice as voters are prone to the same judgmental errors and hence their choices may not be truly random (Kuklinski & Quirk, 2000). Still, regardless of whether the public as a whole is responsive to exogenous events a key question is how individuals navigate themselves in the complex world of politics without extensive political information. Since the majority of citizens know so little about candidate positions, party ideology, or policy implications, how do they decide which candidates or policies to support? To answer this question, political psychologists turned to studies in cognitive psychology, and the concept of **cognitive heuristics**, which soon became one of the most investigated topics in the discipline.

Cognitive heuristics: Mental shortcuts that simplify complex judgments. They reduce cognitive effort but may lead to judgment error.

Cognitive Heuristics

Cognitive heuristics are problem-solving strategies that we use to reach a decision without much effort. In other words, they refer to "a simple procedure that helps find adequate, though often imperfect, answers to difficult questions" (Kahneman, 2011, p. 98) or "methods that use principles of effort-reduction and simplification" (Shah & Oppenheimer, 2008, p. 207). The main idea is straightforward. In our daily lives we are called to make dozens of decisions on both mundane and important issues. These can include for instance which film to watch, whether to attend a party or not, which book to read next, or which university modules to follow next term. These are all examples of choices that we make under limited information. They all involve a degree of uncertainty regarding the returns that we will receive from each outcome. We don't know if the film we chose will end up being terrible or the module will end up being boring. With each decision, we are taking a small risk.

A strategy to minimize this risk would be to collect as much information as possible before reaching a decision. For instance, before going to the cinema one could read every review of the movie available to make sure that the film is worth watching. This strategy, however, does not make much sense. It requires much time and effort and it's simply not worth it for a movie night. Instead, most people choose to watch a film because a friend recommended it, the protagonist is a big star, or simply because they found the film poster intriguing. This is an example of decision-making based on heuristics: We reduce the cognitive effort and time cost involved in reaching a decision by employing strategies aimed at simplifying the task at hand. There are many different types of heuristics, some of which are also relevant to political decision-making. This chapter discusses these next.

The Availability Heuristic

People use heuristics both to make decisions (as in the film example discussed above) and to estimate unknown quantities and the likelihood of uncertain events (Tversky & Kahneman, 1973, 1974). For example, in one of their estimation experiments, Daniel Kahneman and Amos Tversky, two pioneers in the study of heuristics, asked participants the following question: "Suppose you sample a word at random from an English text. Is it more likely that the word starts with a K, or that K is its third letter?"(Tversky & Kahneman, 1973, p. 211). This is admittedly a very hard guess. How would you start answering this? Most people employed a heuristic: They substituted this question with an easier one. They would compare how many words they could easily come up with that start with a K compared to how many words they could think of that have K as their third letter. The first category of words is much easier to bring up compared to the second. Hence most answered that it is most likely to find a word that starts with a K.

This is an example of the **availability heuristic** or in other words the estimation of frequency or probability "by the ease with which instances or associations could be brought to mind" (Tversky & Kahneman, 1973, p. 208). When people are asked to assess the probability of an event, they often rely on how easy it is to think of examples of the event happening. Similarly, they assess the importance of an event based on how easy it is to

Availability heuristic: A cognitive shortcut whereby people assess the importance or frequency of an outcome based on how easily relevant examples come to mind.

recall. The availability heuristic is particularly important in understanding mass media effects in political behavior. For instance, when people are asked to identify the most important problem in the country, they are likely to respond with issues recently covered in the media, which are more easily available in memory (e.g., Iyengar & Kinder, 2010). Similarly, when they are called to evaluate candidates, they are more likely to place greater weight on topics which are overrepresented in the media (Iyengar & Kinder, 2010). When the news focuses more on immigration, voters are more likely to evaluate candidates based on the issue, while when the news prioritizes foreign policy, voters are likely to follow suit. In summary, we are more likely to perceive something as frequent or important based on how easy it is to bring it to mind. Of course, the fact that something is more accessible in memory does not necessarily mean it is indeed more frequent. You are almost twice more likely to find words in which K is the third letter, compared to words that start with a K in a typical English text.

The Representativeness Heuristic

Perhaps the most important heuristic for political decision-making is the representativeness heuristic. The **representativeness heuristic** describes the strategy of "selecting or ordering outcomes by the degree to which the outcomes represent the essential features of the evidence" (Kahneman & Tversky, 1973, p. 238). The representativeness heuristic refers to predicting the probability of an outcome (e.g., a candidate winning a presidential election) based on representativeness (e.g., how representative the candidate is of typical presidents). The representativeness heuristic describes the human tendency to draw heavily on the use of stereotypes to reach a decision, while ignoring other key information. Tversky and Kahneman designed a series of intriguing experiments that illustrate how the representativeness heuristic leads to biases in human decision-making (e.g., Kahneman, 2011). These experiments typically ask participants to make a judgment of an outcome based on a stereotypical description. Consider this classic example from Kahneman (2011, p. 151). "You see a person reading the New York Times on the New York subway. Which of the following is a better bet about the reading stranger? A. She has a PhD B. She does not have a college degree". The representativeness heuristic would lead someone to guess that this person is more likely to hold a PhD, because there is a stereotype that the New York Times is read by the highly educated. However, this is not a sensible choice: Only 2 per cent of the US population holds a PhD degree, while the majority does not have a university

> **Representativeness heuristic**: Assessing the likelihood of an outcome based on how closely it resembles a prototype or stereotype.

degree. Hence, statistically speaking, the person is much more likely not to have a college degree compared to a PhD.

The representativeness heuristic is particularly important when it comes to understanding political decision-making. A prominent example is party affiliation (Lodge & Hamill, 1986; Rahn, 1993). By relying on the representativeness heuristic voters can reasonably infer that candidates of a specific party are representative of the politicians of this party. Hence a voter does not need to have extensive information over a candidate's platform, biography, or the posts that they previously held in order to have a reasonably accurate sense of the policies they stand for and what kind of politician they would be if elected in office. By relying on the representativeness heuristic, they can relatively safely reject a candidate running for a disliked party and consider voting for a candidate running for a liked party. A very similar heuristic is candidate ideology that offers important cues to voters over the candidate's issue positions (Conover & Feldman, 1989). However, party cues have limits on their effectiveness. It is not unusual for politicians to adopt policy positions that bring them at odds with their party. Further, sometimes political parties have different wings that take different policy positions, as is the case for instance with the UK Labour Party, where there exists a left-wing and a moderate faction.

Candidate demographics and style may also convey a large amount of information, as demographic and personality characteristics sometimes reflect stereotypes and evoke decision-making based on the representativeness heuristic. Indeed, many voters form immediate impressions on the representativeness of a candidate for social and ideological groups based on visible characteristics such as age, gender, ethnic background (e.g., Riggle et al., 1992). According to political scientist Samuel Popkin, "personal data gathered from observing a candidate generates a story about the candidate – what he or she is like and is likely to do if elected" (1994, p. 78). Other studies suggest that citizens also tend to form immediate first impressions or "gut" reactions about the personality of a candidate based on their appearance beyond gender, age, or race. For instance, physical attractiveness (which is often associated with positive traits such as competence or friendliness) has been found to boost popularity and vote intentions (Carrión-Yaguana & Carroll, 2023). This is especially the case in low-salience contests where voters do not have much information over the candidates and in elections where voters cast a ballot for a candidate rather than a party (Banducci et al., 2008; Stockemer & Praino, 2017).

Other Examples of Heuristics in Political Behavior

What are other heuristics that citizens employ to navigate themselves in the complex realm of political affairs? One is **party identification**, which refers to an enduring psychological attachment to a political party that shapes political perceptions and preferences (Campbell et al., 1960). Party identification is one of the most common heuristics in political judgment. For example, voters may decide whether to vote or not for an unknown candidate based on the party that supports them (Mondak, 1993). Similarly, they may easily figure out their minds on whether to support or oppose a complex and unknown policy proposal on the basis of which party supports or which party opposes this policy proposal (Popkin, 1994). This is indeed a time-saving strategy that most of the time leads to the same decision voters would have made if they had spent a lot of time reading about the issue positions of an unknown candidate or learning about the content of a complex policy.

Party identification: An enduring psychological attachment with a political party that shapes political perceptions, attitudes, and voting behavior.

Another important heuristic that voters use is the **likability heuristic** (Sniderman, 2000; Sniderman et al., 1993). This heuristic helps citizens to make an educated guess on party and ideological group positions based on their feelings toward these groups (e.g., liberals and conservatives). Average voters may not know much about ideological concepts or policies but they do know which political groups they like and which ones they dislike. By relying on their positive or negative evaluations, they can make educated guesses on where liberals and conservatives stand on different political issues. In other words, "follow the rule of predicting what others believe by taking account of what you believe, weighted by your feelings toward them, and you will be right, by and large" (Sniderman et al., 1993, p. 93). By linking preferable policies with one's own ideological or partisan group and unpreferable policies with the ideologically opposing group, one is able to make a reasonable guess of where two opposing parties stand on issues even without having much political information.

A third key information shortcut, which is often used when it comes to the development of political attitudes on welfare benefits, immigration, and social care is the **deservingness heuristic** (Hansen, 2019; Petersen, 2012; Sniderman et al., 1993). This heuristic simplifies complex policy decisions based on a simple evaluation: Are recipients deserving of the resources allocated to them? If the answer is positive, then state intervention is supported; if not then it is rejected. The deservingness heuristic is closely tied with an attribution of responsibility for one's fate: Is the recipient of help lazy or unlucky? In cases where citizens perceive a misgiving to be one's own fault, they are more likely to decide that they are undeserving of help, while in cases

Deservingness heuristic: A heuristic that simplifies decisions on social aid on the basis of whether the recipient is seen as unlucky (and hence deserving of help) or lazy (and hence undeserving of help).

where the attribution of blame lies outside of individual responsibility, they are more likely to deem the recipient as deserving (Hansen, 2019; Petersen, 2012). Decisions on deservingness are made fast and effortlessly (Petersen et al., 2011). The deservingness heuristic offers a psychological mechanism to explain decision-making processes on a broad array of issues associated with poverty relief, but also key policies aimed at addressing ethnic and racial disparities (Sniderman et al., 1993). It also helps us understand the strong persuasive effect of messages focusing on personal stories – involving either bad luck or laziness – for shaping attitudes toward welfare policies (Aarøe & Petersen, 2020). Studies have shown that opposition to racial equality policies in the United States is shaped by attributions of responsibility for ethnic and racial inequality, and specifically whether inequality is driven by external forces or by lack of effort (Sniderman et al., 1993). Others show that economic migrants are often seen as less deserving than political refugees, which partly explains the gap in support for these two groups (Hager & Veit, 2019). Left-wing and right-wing voters differ on their notions of deservingness, with liberals generally being more likely to be willing to allocate resources (Skitka & Tetlock, 1993). That said, studies have found that the deservingness heuristic plays a role above and beyond ideology (Jensen & Petersen, 2017).

The Low Information Rationality Perspective

We discussed the many strategies that voters can rely on to assess which policies to support or oppose and which politicians to vote for in the absence of extensive political information (see Table 7.1 for an overview). Heuristic devices such as representativeness, likability, or deservingness allow citizens to cut corners when it comes to reasoning over political affairs, saving them a lot of time and effort. Research on heuristics in political behavior challenged the image of the ignorant voter that was drawn by the first political behavior studies of the 1960s. In the 1990s, a group of scholars took the research on heuristics a step further, arguing that voters can rely on heuristics so successfully that they can to a large extent reach the same conclusions they would have reached if they had spent more time collecting information over a political issue. This perspective is called the "low information rationality perspective" in political psychology (Lupia, 1994; Popkin, 1994).

Low information rationality perspective: A theoretical approach arguing that citizens with low levels of political knowledge can still reach accurate political decisions by relying on heuristics.

Low information rationalists argue that much of the encyclopedic knowledge that citizens are asked about in political knowledge surveys is superfluous. Popkin argued that everyday citizens collect a wealth of political information indirectly through their

Table 7.1 Examples of Heuristics in Political Decision-Making

Heuristic	*What Is It?*	*How Does It Work?*	*Example*
Availability	A heuristic that assesses the importance or frequency of outcomes based on how easily examples or information can be recalled from memory.	People infer that if something is easily accessible in memory, it must be important.	Voters disproportionately evaluate candidates based on issues that have been frequently or recently covered in the media, as these are more easily accessible in memory.
Representativeness	A heuristic that involves judging the probability of an outcome on how closely it matches a stereotype or prototype.	People infer candidates' political ideology or electability by assessing how representative the candidates are of that category.	A voter infers that a candidate from a political party is representative of politicians from this party, ignoring the candidate's ideological beliefs and record.
Party identification	An enduring psychological affiliation with a specific party. Works as a perceptual screen for understanding the political world.	Voters readily accept the policies or candidates of the party they identify with without paying much attention to the content of the policy or the candidate themselves.	If a party a voter identifies with supports a policy, the voter is likely to perceive it as a good policy without knowing much about it.
Likability	A heuristic based on affective evaluations of candidates, parties, or social groups.	Voters infer policy positions by projecting their own preferences onto liked groups, and preferences they disagree with onto disliked groups.	A voter assumes that a liked party supports a policy they favor without really knowing the party's actual stance.
Deservingness	A heuristic that evaluates policies based on whether recipients are deserving of help or not.	Narrows down decision-making on the basis of whether a group or individual is perceived to deserve help.	Disability benefits are more popular than unemployment benefits, because for some, the unemployed are deemed deserving of their fate.

daily lives (1994). For instance, people notice through their daily interactions whether inflation has increased, whether petrol prices are going up, or whether unemployment or crime has increased in their area. This information interacts with information they gather from the mass media, which allows voters to assess whether these issues reflect national trends: "Thus, they do not need to know which party controls Congress, or the names of their senators, in order to know something about the state of the economy or proposed cuts in Social Security" (Popkin, 1994, p. 213). Some studies offer evidence for the low rationality argument. Lupia conducted a seminal study on the use of heuristics in the context of a complex insurance reform ballot in California. He chose the topic specifically because of its complexity and the lack of available party cues that would help voters decide where they stand. He found that voters who had low information over the issue they were called to vote on but could correctly identify the insurance's industry position (which they used as an information shortcut) were arriving at the same vote choice as voters with high levels of knowledge on the issue (1994). This shows, according to the author, that simple heuristics may allow voters to act in the same way as they would have if they had taken the time and effort to collect extensive information over a political issue.

This low information rationality perspective, however, has also received criticism. First, as Delli-Carpini and Keeter remind, "the heuristic model is based on *low* information rationality, not *no* information rationality" (1996, p. 52). This means that some political information is needed in order to make effective use of cognitive heuristics. Using the likability heuristic, for example, requires extensive information on party positions on key issues and one's own stance on these issues. Making an educated guess of a candidate's policies by their physical appearance requires knowledge on the sociodemographic composition of different parties. In fact, some heuristics such as endorsements or candidate ideology are mostly used by those with high – rather than low – levels of political knowledge (Lau & Redlawsk, 2001; Sniderman et al., 1993). In other words "Political sophisticates' comparative advantage is not that they have a stupendous amount of knowledge, but that they know how to get the most out of the knowledge they do possess" (Sniderman et al., 1993, p. 24).

Second, there has been increasing evidence that the politically sophisticated and unsophisticated differ. Voters with high levels of political knowledge are better able to adjust policy preferences and vote choices to their beliefs, political values, and self-interest (e.g., Andersen et al., 2005; Bartels, 2016). In fact, some research cites the lack of political knowledge of mass publics as a key reason behind the endorsement of economically inegalitarian policies by disadvantaged voters (Macdonald, 2020). For instance, in the US context, Bartels investigated mass support for the 2001 and 2003 tax cuts signed by President Bush, which were economic programs that included the cut of the top rate tax and introduced tax reductions on dividends and stock profits (2016). Bartels observed that among supporters of the tax cuts were citizens who also answered that the rich are asked to pay too little in tax and were concerned about the levels of economic inequality. He further found that opposition to the tax cut only appeared among voters with economically left-wing values who had the necessary political knowledge to understand the relevance of the tax plan for economic inequality to their own values (2016, p. 128). In sum, while it is true that cognitive heuristics are useful in helping voters, political knowledge still matters for the quality of political decision-making.

Conclusion

How does democracy work when citizens are called to decide on complex policy issues but most of them lack political information? Answering this paradox has occupied a very large part of political psychology literature. The first studies showing that levels of political knowledge were woefully low in mass publics brought much pessimism over the ability of mass publics to provide meaningful inputs to policymakers. This somber depiction of mass publics as ignorant decision-makers was restored with the advent of a large stream of studies showing that cognitive heuristics can go a long way to help people reach complex decisions with relative accuracy. Optimism over citizens' political competence peaked in the 1990s when some scholars argued that many politically unknowledgeable voters end up supporting the same policies they would have if they had more political information, so extensive political knowledge was not necessarily needed to reach meaningful political decisions. Subsequent research added important nuance to these findings. Indeed, citizens tend to rely heavily on cognitive heuristics, such as party identification, likability, deservingness, or even candidate appearance, to decide on issues or elections they know little about, but heuristics can often lead to erroneous judgments, especially by the ones who need them most: those who lack political knowledge.

Further Reading

Colombo, C., & Steenbergen, M. R. (2020). Heuristics and biases in political decision making. In *Oxford research encyclopedia of politics*. Oxford: Oxford University Press. A review chapter presenting additional research evidence on the role of heuristics in political decision-making processes.

Kahneman, D. (2011). *Thinking, fast and slow*. New York: Farrar, Straus and Giroux. An accessible, popular science book presenting a fascinating overview of Kahneman and Tversky's research on heuristics.

References

Aarøe, L., & Petersen, M. B. (2020). Cognitive biases and communication strength in social networks: The case of episodic frames. *British Journal of Political Science*, *50*(4), 1561–1581.

Andersen, R., Tilley, J., & Heath, A. F. (2005). Political knowledge and enlightened preferences: Party choice through the electoral cycle. *British Journal of Political Science*, *35* (2), 285–302.

Banducci, S. A., Karp, J. A., Thrasher, M., & Rallings, C. (2008). Ballot photographs as cues in low-information elections. *Political Psychology*, *29* (6), 903–917.

Bartels, L. M. (2016). *Unequal democracy: The political economy of the new gilded age*. Princeton: Princeton University Press.

Campbell, A., Converse, P. E., Miller, W. E., & Stokes, D. E. (1960). *The American voter*. Chicago, IL: University of Chicago Press.

Carrión-Yaguana, V. D., & Carroll, R. (2023). The effects of candidate appearance on electoral success: Evidence from Ecuador. *Political Research Quarterly*, *76* (3), 1168–1179.

Converse, P. (1964). The nature of belief systems in mass publics. In D. Apter (Ed.), *Ideology and discontent* (pp. 206–261). New York: The Free Press.

Conover, P. J., & Feldman, S. (1989). Candidate perception in an ambiguous world: Campaigns, cues, and inference processes. *American Journal of Political Science*, *33* (4), 912–940.

Delli Carpini, M. X., & Keeter, S. (1996). *What Americans know about politics and why it matters*. New Haven: Yale University Press.

Downs, A. (1957). *An economic theory of democracy*. New York: Harper and Row.

Jensen, C., & Petersen, M. B. (2017). The deservingness heuristic and the politics of health care. *American Journal of Political Science*, *61* (1), 68–83.

Hager, A., & Veit, S. (2019). Attitudes toward asylum seekers: Evidence from Germany. *Public Opinion Quarterly*, *83* (2), 412–422.

Hansen, K. J. (2019). Who cares if they need help? The deservingness heuristic, humanitarianism, and welfare opinions. *Political Psychology*, *40* (2), 413–430.

Iyengar, S., & Kinder, D. R. (2010). *News that matters: Television and American Opinion*. Chicago, IL: University of Chicago Press.

Kahneman, D., & Tversky, A. (1973). On the psychology of prediction. *Psychological Review*, *80* (4), 237–251.

Kuklinski, J. H., & Quirk, P. J. (2000). Reconsidering the rational public: Cognition, heuristics, and mass opinion. In A. Lupia, M. D. McCubbins, & S. L. Popkin (Eds.), *Elements of reason: Cognition, choice, and the bounds of rationality* (pp. 153–182). Cambridge: Cambridge University Press.

Lau, R. R., & Redlawsk, D. P. (2001). Advantages and disadvantages of cognitive heuristics in political decision making. *American Journal of Political Science*, *45* (4), 951–971.

Lippmann, W. (1922). *Public opinion*. New York: Harcourt, Brace.

Lodge, M., & Hamill, R. (1986). A partisan schema for political information processing. *American Political Science Review*, *80* (2), 505–519.

Lupia, A. (1994). Shortcuts versus encyclopedias: Information and voting behavior in California insurance reform elections. *American Political Science Review*, *88* (1), 63–76.

Macdonald, D. (2020). Class attitudes, political knowledge, and support for redistribution in an era of inequality. *Social Science Quarterly*, *101* (2), 960–977.

Mondak, J. J. (1993). Public opinion and heuristic processing of source cues. *Political Behavior*, *15*, 167–192.

Page, B. I., & Shapiro, R. Y. (1992). *The rational public: Fifty years of trends in Americans' policy preferences*. Chicago: University of Chicago Press.

Petersen, M. B. (2012). Social welfare as small-scale help: Evolutionary psychology and the deservingness heuristic. *American Journal of Political Science, 56* (1), 1–16.

Petersen, M. B., Slothuus, R., Stubager, R., & Togeby, L. (2011). Deservingness versus values in public opinion on welfare: The automaticity of the deservingness heuristic. *European Journal of Political Research, 50* (1), 24–52.

Popkin, S. L. (1994). *The reasoning voter: Communication and persuasion in presidential campaigns.* Chicago, IL: University of Chicago Press.

Rahn, W. M. (1993). The role of partisan stereotypes in information processing about political candidates. *American Journal of Political Science, 37* (2), 472–496.

Riggle, E. D., Ottati, V. C., Wyer Jr, R. S., Kuklinski, J., & Schwarz, N. (1992). Bases of political judgments: The role of stereotypic and nonstereotypic information. *Political Behavior, 14* (1), 67–87.

Shah, A. K., & Oppenheimer, D. M. (2008). Heuristics made easy: An effort-reduction framework. *Psychological Bulletin, 134* (2), 207.

Skitka, L. J., & Tetlock, P. E. (1993). Providing public assistance: Cognitive and motivational processes underlying liberal and conservative policy preferences. *Journal of Personality and Social Psychology, 65* (6), 1205.

Sniderman, P. M. (2000). Taking sides: A fixed choice theory of political reasoning. In A. Lupia, M. D. McCubbins, & S. L. Popkin (Eds.), *Elements of reason: Cognition, choice, and the bounds of rationality* (pp. 67–84). Cambridge: Cambridge University Press.

Sniderman, P. M., Brody, R. A., & Tetlock, P. E. (1993). *Reasoning and choice: Explorations in political psychology.* Cambridge: Cambridge University Press.

Stockemer, D., & Praino, R. (2017). Physical attractiveness, voter heuristics and electoral systems: The role of candidate attractiveness under different institutional designs. *The British Journal of Politics and International Relations, 19* (2), 336–352.

Tversky, A., & Kahneman, D. (1973). Availability: A heuristic for judging frequency and probability. *Cognitive Psychology, 5* (2), 207–232.

Tversky, A., & Kahneman, D. (1974). Judgment under uncertainty: Heuristics and biases: Biases in judgments reveal some heuristics of thinking under uncertainty. *Science, 185* (4157), 1124–1131.

Chapter 8

Emotions in Political Behavior

> When a man is a prey to his emotions, he is not his own master, but lies at the mercy of fortune: so much so, that he is often compelled, while seeing that which is better for him to follow that which is worse.
>
> Benedict de Spinoza, *The Ethics IV: Of Human Bondage, or the Strength of the Emotions*, p. 3

This quote from the 17th-century Dutch philosopher Baruch Spinoza sounds intuitive to us today. From an early age, we are taught that emotions can lead to poor decisions, driving us toward irrational goals or pushing us into hasty choices that we come to regret once calm returns and reason is restored. Not acting on our emotions is often good advice. When we pursue a goal with exaggerated enthusiasm we may act in a careless way. When we experience anger, we may say hurtful things that we later regret. And exaggerated fear in the form of phobias often leads us to unreasonably sense danger in places and situations where there is none. The seeming contradiction between rationality and emotion has been central to human thought. Sometimes the distinction is epitomized in spatial terms with logic placed in the brain and emotions placed in the heart. The brain is portrayed as facilitating deliberation and reason, while the heart is portrayed as encouraging our irrational impulses.

Bearing in mind the deep-held conviction that emotion is an enemy of reason, it is not hard to see why the study of emotions was largely left out of political research at its inception. Emotions for most political scientists were seen as alien and contradictory to the political process. They were deemed obscure, mysterious, and irrational processes that were both hard to define and measure (Marcus, 2013). Importantly, according to this view, emotions obstruct citizens from engaging in logical reasoning, which ought to constitute the cornerstone of the political calculus and deliberation in a democracy (Marcus, 2013).

It is only relatively recently that political psychology has moved away from these conceptualizations of emotions. Nowadays, we treat emotions as a very useful tool for understanding the psychological motivations of a wide range

DOI: 10.4324/9781003460084-10

of political behaviors. Indeed, the number of articles on emotions and politics has increased exponentially not only as a result of the growing interdisciplinary dialogue between political science and psychology but also because of the numerous different threats that many societies face today. Terrorism, pandemics, climate change, demographic change, and growing economic inequality, all evoke strong emotional reactions. And as we will see shortly, these emotional responses bear significant implications for mass political choices. The rest of this chapter presents a set of key theories that have dominated the field of political psychology: Hot Cognition, Cognitive Appraisal Theories, and the Theory of Affective Intelligence. This chapter ends by presenting an overview of how specific emotions – fear, anger, disgust, and hope – impact upon political behavior.

Hot Cognition and Motivated Reasoning

Hot cognition: A hypothesis that argues that emotion and cognition are inseparable in judgment and that in many instances our political reasoning is caused by our emotions rather than being a product of unbiased processing of information.

Hot Cognition theory posits that emotion and cognition are inexorably entwined and impossible to separate. Even if this sounds counterintuitive, the theory (in its simplest form) is relatively straightforward. The hot cognition hypothesis states that all political objects that we have encountered in the past are affectively charged. When we first come across new candidates, parties, policies, or social movements, we form an initial affective evaluation based on the first information we collect about them ("I like them", "I trust them", etc.). This affective evaluation is then stored in long-term memory (Lodge et al., 1989). However, the specific information that contributed to our initial evaluation is most of the time quickly forgotten as it is simply too costly for our brains to keep all the relevant information in our long-term memory (Lodge et al., 1995; Lodge & Taber, 2005). Hence, often voters like or dislike politicians without really remembering why. Each time we encounter the object again, for example, when we watch the news or discuss politics with our friends, the affective impression ("I like this" or "I hate this") is retrieved from long-term memory within milliseconds. Simply mentioning politicians (Trump, Modi), policies ("Welfare state"; "net zero"), or movements ("#metoo") automatically evoke emotion and information.

When we encounter new information, we update our attitudes toward political objects positively or negatively. However, the processing of this new information takes place in a biased manner because it depends on our prior

> **Motivated reasoning:** The selective processing of political information to reach a preferred conclusion.

positive or negative feelings about the object. For instance, when we dislike a candidate and we encounter new information about them we will process this information in a way that integrates it into our existing dislike for them (Redlawsk, 2002). This helps us understand why people usually do not equally consider messages from all ideological sides with an open mind, nor do they necessarily update their opinions in the light of new information. On the contrary, people process new political information in a way that upholds pre-existing evaluations and conclusions. This is a key claim of **motivated reasoning theory**, which is based on the hot cognition hypothesis.

Motivated reasoning theory argues that when exposed to new information people have two competing motives: accuracy goals and directional goals (Taber & Lodge, 2006). Accuracy goals motivate people to carefully consider information in order to reach an impartial and accurate conclusion. If reasoning was governed solely by accuracy goals, the reception of credible new information that challenges a pre-existing conclusion would lead to attitude change. Directional goals, however, motivate people to selectively process new information to uphold a pre-existing conclusion. Hence, they consider that evidence and arguments which align with their existing attitudes, beliefs, and worldviews are more compelling than evidence and arguments which challenge them. For example, consider two people with different ideological leanings reading an article by a credible academic arguing that increasing income taxes for the very rich would reduce economic inequality without affecting growth. An economically conservative citizen who strongly opposes high taxation would be likely to dismiss the conclusions of the article either by countering the arguments presented or dismissing the source. A left-wing citizen on the other hand would readily accept the information presented there as it is in line with their prior political beliefs.

Hot cognition theories help us understand why people are biased toward the political information they encounter. However, these perspectives have received criticism on the basis that they treat emotion as either positive or negative (Brader & Marcus, 2013). We either like a politician, a group, or a policy or we dislike them. Yet, different negative emotions may have wholly different behavioral consequences. For example, anxiety and anger are both negative emotions. Yet, if we are scared of someone, we will try to stay out of their way, while if we are angry, we will likely seek to approach and confront them. Many political psychologists realized that distinguishing between different emotions may offer additional nuance in understanding the psychological motivations of political behavior. This has led them to turn to psychological theories of emotions called **Cognitive Appraisal Theories**. Instead of taxonomizing affect as simply positive or negative, these theories aim at investigating the conditions under which we experience a wide range of different emotions and the impact that these emotions have on our behavior.

Cognitive Appraisal Theories: A group of theories positing that emotional reactions are a product of interpretations (appraisals) of an event for an individual and that different appraisals produce different emotions.

Cognitive Appraisal Theories

Rather than relying on a simple valence of like versus dislike, Cognitive Appraisal Theories present a more elaborate taxonomy of emotion. The main idea is that different interpretations of a stimulus evoke different emotional reactions, or in other words, that humans experience emotions after they appraise a situation (e.g., Smith & Ellsworth, 1985).

Even though scholars have proposed different types of appraisals, they are generally divided into two broad types: primary and secondary. **Primary appraisals** concern the relevance of the stimulus to our goals or well-being. To put it differently, the first appraisals concern whether the stimulus is something worth experiencing emotion about or not and, if it is, whether it is something pleasant or unpleasant (Lazarus, 1991; Smith & Ellsworth, 1985). **Secondary appraisals** are more precise. They concern a person's options to cope with the emotional target or as Lazarus explains "What, if anything, can I do in this encounter and how will what I do and what is going to happen affect my well-being?" (1991, p. 134). Secondary appraisals include attribution of blame, that is, whether we or someone else is to credit or blame for an event. When, for example, someone else is responsible for an unpleasant event, we are more likely to experience anger. When the same event is our own fault we will experience guilt or shame. Other secondary appraisals concern whether the individual thinks they have the potential to cope with the situation and whether they believe that a possible action can change the situation for the better.

Note that appraisals are not fixed and emotions can change as the brain constantly appraises and reappraises the social environment. To highlight the appraisal process with an example, imagine walking in a corridor at your university and suddenly feel someone push you. How would you feel? Primary appraisals have already taken place as this is something both important to your well-being and unpleasant. The secondary appraisals will take place once you turn your head around to appraise the situation. If you realize that the push was meant as a distasteful joke by a fellow student you will probably experience anger. If you turn around and see a gorilla you will almost certainly experience fear. The difference is the perpetrator and your coping potential against them. The fellow student is familiar and is a threat that you can likely overcome (by filing a complaint for instance). On the other hand, most people would feel unable to cope with the threat posed by a gorilla, hence they will experience fear instead of anger.

Affective Intelligence Theory

Affective Intelligence Theory: A political decision-making theory based on emotion. It argues that when the disposition system (associated with enthusiasm) is active, people rely on past habits to guide their decision-making, while when the surveillance system (associated with anxiety) is active they tend to engage in deliberative processes.

Disposition system: An affective subsystem that operates in normal and familiar situations. It increases reliance on political dispositions (such as party identification) for decision-making processes. It is part of Affective Intelligence Theory.

Cognitive heuristic: Problem-solving strategies that we use to reach a decision without much effort (see also Chapter 7).

One of the most central political psychology theories is **Affective Intelligence Theory** (Marcus et al., 2000). It aims at providing a framework that helps us understand how emotion is associated with the acquisition of political information and behavioral change. Its main claim is that emotions condition how attentive individuals are to politics and whether they are likely to question their partisan and ideological attachments or stick to them.

Affective Intelligence Theory postulates that individuals rely on two largely subconscious affective subsystems that help them reach decisions. Each of the two subsystems corresponds to different behavioral repertoires. The first system is called the **disposition system**. This system is active in mundane and habitual circumstances, managing reliance on routine behaviors that individuals do not spend time or effort thinking about. During calm times people tend to make decisions without overly thinking about them. An example of the disposition system at play in politics is partisanship. As we discussed in Chapter 7, partisanship is a key **cognitive heuristic**. It allows voters to reach political decisions without investing in effort to acquire political information when choosing to agree or disagree with a policy or who to vote for in the next election by relying on previously learned strategies. However, relying on habit is an ineffective strategy when dealing with novel or threatening situations. This is when the second system, called the **surveillance system**, is activated. The surveillance system identifies circumstances that involve unfamiliarity or threat. In these instances, it interrupts habitual behavior strategies and motivates conscious action. By activating conscious awareness and enhancing information-seeking processes over the stimulus, the surveillance system leads to effortful, thoughtful consideration of what the best course of action is in order to overcome the threat. An example of the surveillance system in politics is the acquisition of political information about an upcoming election or the careful consideration of party candidates and the important issues that are at stake.

> **Surveillance system**: An affective subsystem which becomes activated in threatening or unfamiliar situations. It interrupts reliance on habitual responses and motivates individuals to seek information on how to cope with the threat. It is part of Affective Intelligence Theory.

According to the theory, the successful execution of familiar and habitual tasks elicits enthusiasm and increases reliance on the disposition system. On the other hand, situations that involve unfamiliar threats or uncertainty elicit anxiety, which signifies to the brain that we need to pay attention so as to overcome the threat or, in other words, that the surveillance system needs to be activated. This is an interesting point as the theory attributes the processes that are most often associated with rational and deliberative decision-making to anxiety rather than emotional calmness.

The Effects of Specific Emotions on Political Behavior

Political psychology research in the last two decades has investigated the effects of specific emotional states on different aspects of political choice. These effects can either be direct, where the experience of a specific emotion renders some political outcomes more desirable than others, or indirect, where emotions influence the criteria we use to make political decisions. Finally, a third stream of research has looked into how discrete emotions affect our willingness to participate in politics in different ways. Political psychologists have explored the impact of emotional reactions that are commonly experienced in politics, including fear, anger, disgust, enthusiasm, and hope. In the next section I summarize the key findings for each of these different affective reactions.

Anxiety and Fear

Unlike other subfields in psychology that would argue that fear and anxiety constitute separate emotional reactions (e.g., Grillon, 2008), the two are largely treated as synonymous and are typically used interchangeably in political psychology research. It has been found that the semantic terms "anxious", "fearful", "worried", and "scared" show very high correlations in mass surveys making them practically indistinguishable (Marcus et al., 2017). Fear is elicited when people find themselves exposed to novel and unfamiliar circumstances, there is no clear attribution of blame, and they have limited coping potential against the threat (Lazarus, 1991). Economic recessions, climate change, terror attacks, and pandemics are all threats that have been found to evoke strong fearful reactions in mass publics (Albertson & Gadarian, 2015; Vasilopoulos et al., 2023).

Fear has been one of the earliest and the most studied emotions in political psychology. Research has found that it affects three political behavior domains. First, it enhances information-seeking processes. Second, fear is associated with attitude change and reliance on contemporaneous assessments to decide on political issues. These two claims are posited by the Affective Intelligence Theory described above. Finally, fear directly impacts upon political preferences, rendering citizens more prone to endorsing risk-aversive and protective policies in order to address a threat (Vasilopoulos et al., 2019).

The association of fear and motivation to seek out information about the threatening stimulus has been studied extensively. Most studies find evidence of a positive effect of fear on the motivation to search for political information (Albertson & Gadarian, 2015; MacKuen et al., 2010; Vasilopoulos, 2018; Valentino et al., 2008). What is less straightforward is the type of information that people seek when they are anxious. Some find that anxious individuals are more likely to look for information that directly addresses the issue they are worried about (Valentino et al., 2008) even if it comes from ideologically opposing sources (MacKuen et al., 2010). Others find that anxiety promotes a biased information search in favor of threatening information (Albertson & Gadarian, 2015). Anxiety has also been found to be negatively associated with recalling information, thus having a deleterious effect on actual political learning (Huddy et al., 2005).

The second main quality of anxiety is that it renders citizens more likely to abandon their partisan or ideological dispositions and update their political attitudes in the light of new information (Brader, 2005; Marcus et al., 2000). This is one of the main claims of the Affective Intelligence Theory. There is much evidence that anxiety in the light of exogenous shocks such as terror attacks, climate change, or the Covid-19 pandemic leads to opinion change (Albertson & Gadarian, 2015; Nai et al., 2017). Nai and colleagues, for instance, found that anxiety following exposure to scientific information about global warming renders one more supportive of policies that tackle climate change (Nai et al., 2017).

This behavioral quality of anxiety has crucial implications for understanding political decision-making processes. Earlier we mentioned that citizens tend to be biased information processors, evaluating political information and arguments based on pre-existing partisan and ideological attachments. Motivated reasoning theory argues that citizens readily accept information that agrees with a preferred conclusion, and try hard to think of possible flaws when they are exposed to arguments that oppose a preferred conclusion (e.g., Taber & Lodge, 2006). It has been found however that anxiety can break this cycle: when voters encounter enough negative information to make them anxious, they break away from motivated reasoning processes, becoming more open to opinion change when exposed to new information (Redlawsk et al., 2010). In sum, these studies suggest that anxiety may lead to more open decision-making patterns that rely less on partisan or ideological convictions (MacKuen et al., 2010).

However, it is important to note that while anxiety leads people to change their minds on a political issue, at the same time it motivates them to support policies or candidates that offer protection from the threat. In other words, anxiety does not open the door evenly to an endless realm of political choice but – in line with its risk-aversive properties – leads individuals toward protective and risk-free policy options. When people experience anxiety, they tend to perceive threats as serious, and they try to navigate themselves as cautiously as possible to protect themselves. When it comes to politics, several studies have identified a link between experiencing anxiety and support for conservative, authoritarian and liberty-restricting policies (Albertson & Gadarian, 2015; Vasilopoulos et al., 2023).

Anger

Anger is elicited in situations where goals are obstructed or norms are violated, there is a clear attribution of blame, and the perceiver feels that they have the ability to cope with the threat (Lazarus, 1991; Lerner & Keltner, 2001). Interestingly, even though anger is a negative emotion, it is associated with optimistic perceptions of one's ability to punish the object of anger. Anger in politics has, by and large, opposite behavioral patterns compared to fear. Whereas fear is associated with information search, attitude change, and preference for risk-aversive and protective policies, anger inhibits information-seeking tendencies, renders citizens more likely to double down and decide on the basis of what they already know, and boosts preferences for aggressive and risk-seeking options in order to address a threat.

Anger is an emotion that motivates action rather than information seeking or deliberation. Even though anger may increase attention to politics, it impedes information seeking and political learning processes (MacKuen et al., 2010; Valentino et al., 2008). Consequently, anger is associated with haphazard decision-making strategies such as increased reliance on heuristics (Bodenhausen et al., 1994). Moreover, anger has been found to bolster ideological bias when it comes to processing new information (Suhay & Erisen, 2018) and increases reliance on ideological and partisan attachments when it comes to deciding on political issues (MacKuen et al., 2010). The shallow and biased assimilation of information under a state of anger was highlighted in a recent study in South Korea that found that anger bolstered the acceptance and spreading of pseudoscientific information about the Covid-19 pandemic, with the effect being stronger among conservatives (Han et al., 2020).

In addition to information processing, there is plenty of empirical evidence that anger boosts various forms of political participation, including electoral registration, turnout, and participation in protests, even those that entail high cost in terms of time or effort or even risk for the individual (Valentino et al., 2011; Vasilopoulos, 2018). A study on the impact of the introduction of voting-ID laws illustrates this point well. Voting-ID laws in the United States have been introduced in some Republican states in order to reduce voter fraud but are largely perceived as a means to demobilize minority voters, who are less likely to hold the identification cards required to register to vote compared to Whites. Normally one should expect that the higher the costs of political participation, the lower the participation rate. Yet what the study found was that anger evoked among Democrats by these laws potently boosted participation and nullified the effect of the extra participation costs (Valentino & Neuner, 2017).

Apart from its impact on participation, research has further found that anger shapes attitudes and vote choices, directly rendering voters more prone to endorsing risky, punitive, or aggressive policies (Huddy et al., 2007). This is in line with studies in psychology that find that anger makes humans more prone to take risks and motivates them to harm the object of anger (Carver & Harmon-Jones, 2009; Lerner & Keltner, 2001). These properties of anger are key as they help us understand the rise of populist candidates and parties in different places around the world. These candidates often rely on a strong emotive rhetoric, claiming that they represent "ordinary citizens" who have been betrayed by the elites (Widmann, 2021). Studies have found that this vindictive, aggressive rhetoric is particularly appealing to the segments of the electorate who experience anger as a result of economic, cultural, or other types of threats (Rhodes-Purdy et al., 2023; Rico et al., 2017; Vasilopoulos et al., 2019).

Disgust

Disgust has only relatively recently attracted scholarly attention in political psychology literature. Past research has treated disgust as a proximate emotional reaction to anger (e.g., Marcus et al., 2000), yet it is becoming increasingly clear that the two have distinct consequences for political behavior. Similar to fear and anger, disgust is evoked in the face of threat, and serves the specific evolutionary function of protecting the individual from disease. The appraisal pattern of disgust is simple as it is elicited in instances where the threatening stimulus involves possible contamination (Lazarus, 1991). Hence, humans respond with disgust toward stimuli that are potentially pathogenic such as body fluids, corpses, insects, or rotten food (Rozin et al., 2016). This reaction also extends to nonconforming physical appearance, skin lesions, or sexual deviance (Georgarakis, 2023). The main behavioral qualities of disgust are avoidance and physical distancing.

Aarøe and her colleagues argue that humans have evolved to be attentive not only to potentially dangerous pathogens but also to unfamiliar groups (Aarøe et al., 2017). In this sense, according to the authors, phenotypical characteristics, such as skin color, may be misperceived as potentially threatening by people prone to experiencing disgust. This behavioral aspect of disgust makes it directly relevant to political behavior. Indeed, a number of studies from different settings have found that those more prone to experiencing disgust are likely to hold negative attitudes toward ethnic minorities and be more in favor of immigration-restricting policies (Aarøe et al., 2017; Clifford et al., 2023; Kam & Estes, 2016; Navarrete & Fessler, 2006). Moreover, individuals scoring high in disgust sensitivity are more likely to hold negative attitudes toward other groups that physically, culturally, or behaviorally deviate from the mainstream, such as LGBTQ community members, the homeless, or people with disabilities (Clifford & Piston, 2017; Kam & Estes, 2016). The psychological motivation here is different compared to authoritarianism or social dominance orientation that we explored in Chapter 3. The mechanism is to keep one's distance from groups that are consciously or unconsciously perceived as potentially harmful for the self, rather than to punish social deviants or dominate low-status groups.

These effects are not confined only to those who are chronically prone to experiencing disgust. A recent study focusing on the Covid-19 pandemic in the United States, for instance, found that experimentally evoking disgust rendered people more likely to say that they would avoid contact with Asian people or agree with preemptive quarantine measures specifically targeting Asians, compared to a control group who did not experience disgust (Georgarakis, 2023). Finally, some research has further investigated the effects of disgust in the realm of political information processing, finding that disgust is associated with information avoidance about the threatening stimulus (Clifford & Jerit, 2018).

Positive Emotions: Enthusiasm and Hope

The most studied positive emotions in political behavior are enthusiasm and hope. Even though these are based on distinct appraisals, some researchers build composite indices of positive emotions that integrate both in a common emotional dimension (Marcus et al., 2000; MacKuen et al., 2010). While both emotions are future-oriented, enthusiasm is generated by the successful execution of tasks and the prospect or achievement of reward (Brader & Marcus, 2013). Hope on the other hand is evoked in threatening and uncertain situations when one is "fearing the worst but yearning for better"

(Lazarus, 1991, p. 282). Both emotions increase efficacy and are associated with optimistic assessments of a situation.

Enthusiasm in politics is often generated in political campaigns or by charismatic leaders (Brader, 2005; Erisen, 2018). It has been found to be impactful when it comes to political information processing, attitude stability, and political participation (Marcus et al., 2000). Similar to anger, enthusiasm increases reliance on past convictions in political decision-making and is associated with resistance to attitude change (Marcus et al., 2000). Enthusiasm has further been found to boost all forms of political participation (Brader, 2005; Marcus et al., 2000). In the case of Turkey, for instance, Erisen (2018) found that enthusiasm greatly increased the propensity to participate in the anti-government Gezi park protest movement above and beyond individual characteristics such as ideology or political interest. It should be noted however that the effect of enthusiasm in political participation tends to be weaker compared to anger (Valentino et al., 2011).

Hope on the other hand is relatively understudied. Some studies have found a positive association between hope and political efficacy and participation, which can be attributed to hope's association with optimism about the probability of a positive outcome (Greenaway et al., 2016; Wlodarczyk et al., 2017). Much of the available research on hope focuses on its potential to motivate compromise and forgiveness following intergroup conflict (Cohen-Chen et al., 2014; Halperin et al., 2008). In the context of the Israel-Palestine conflict, for example, hope (conceptualized as holding simultaneous beliefs that peace is both desirable and attainable) has been found to be associated with support for bi-national peacekeeping initiatives (Leshem & Halperin, 2020).

Conclusion

After decades of neglect, there is now a consensus among political psychologists that emotions offer a potent tool for understanding the psychological motivations of political choice and participation tendencies of mass publics. The first part of this chapter discussed three major theories of emotion. The second part discussed the impact of discrete emotions on political behavior. Table 8.1 presents a summary of how emotions shape political behavior and decision-making criteria. A key takeaway point is that emotions are not in tension with reason as Spinoza, quoted at the beginning of this chapter, and others would argue. On the contrary, emotions such as anxiety may facilitate information gathering and attitude change.

Political psychologists have uncovered a lot about how emotions shape our political choices. Yet there is a lot we still do not know. For example, there is still much to discover on what drives the experience of discrete emotions (e.g., fear instead of anger) and the strength of emotional arousal when exposed to political stimuli (see Bakker et al., 2021). Additionally, more research is needed to understand how differences in emotional experience drive inequalities in political participation. An important study in the United States identified for

Table 8.1 Emotions & Political Behavior

Emotion	*Impact on Political Behavior*	*Impact on Political Decision-Making Criteria*
Fear/anxiety	Preferences for risk-averse & protective policies	Increases information search Attitude change Lower reliance on predispositions
Anger	Preference for risk seeking, aggressive policies & candidates Boosts political participation	Decreases information search Resistance to attitude change More reliance on predispositions
Disgust	Increase in hostility toward minorities, immigrants	Depresses information search
Enthusiasm/hope	Hope motivates reconciliation in intergroup conflict Boosts political participation	More reliance on predispositions

instance that whereas Whites respond to political threat by experiencing anger, African Americans respond with resignation (Phoenix, 2019). Findings like this help to explain and even address gaps in political organization and participation of disadvantaged groups. All in all, emotions are crucial aspects of our decision-making processes and their systematic study can only enrich our understanding of politics.

Further Reading

Damasio, A. R. (2006). *Descartes' error.* New York: Random House. A fascinating popular science account on the relationship that shows how emotion is a prerequisite for rational thought.

Marcus, G. E., Neuman, W. R., & MacKuen, M. (2000). *Affective intelligence and political judgment.* Chicago: University of Chicago Press. A detailed presentation of Affective Intelligence theory.

Rhodes-Purdy, M., Navarre, R., & Utych, S. M. (2023). *The age of discontent: Populism, extremism, and conspiracy theories in contemporary democracies.* Cambridge: Cambridge University Press. This book explains support for far right extremism on the basis of emotional reactions following economic crises.

Webster, S. W., & Albertson, B. (2022). Emotion and politics: Noncognitive psychological biases in public opinion. *Annual Review of Political Science, 25* (1), 401–418. A detailed overview of research on emotions and political behavior.

References

Aarøe, L., Petersen, M. B., & Arceneaux, K. (2017). The behavioral immune system shapes political intuitions: Why and how individual differences in disgust sensitivity underlie opposition to immigration. *American Political Science Review, 111* (2), 277–294.

Albertson, B., & Gadarian, S. K. (2015). *Anxious politics: Democratic citizenship in a threatening world*. Cambridge: Cambridge University Press.
Bakker, B. N., Schumacher, G., & Rooduijn, M. (2021). Hot politics? Affective responses to political rhetoric. *American Political Science Review*, *115* (1), 150–164.
Bodenhausen, G. V., Sheppard, L. A., & Kramer, G. P. (1994). Negative affect and social judgment: The differential impact of anger and sadness. *European Journal of Social Psychology*, *24*, 45–62.
Brader, T. (2005). Striking a responsive chord: How political ads motivate and persuade voters by appealing to emotions. *American Journal of Political Science*,*49* (2), 388–405.
Brader, T., & Marcus, G. E. (2013). Emotion and political psychology. In L. Huddy, D. O. Sears, & J. S. Levy (Eds.), *The Oxford handbook of political psychology* (pp. 165–204). Oxford: Oxford University Press.
Carver, C. S., & Harmon-Jones, E. (2009). Anger is an approach-related affect: Evidence and implications. *Psychological Bulletin*, *135*, 183–204.
Clifford, S., Erisen, C., Wendell, D., & Cantú, F. (2023). Disgust sensitivity and support for immigration across five nations. *Politics and the Life Sciences*, *42* (1), 65–80.
Clifford, S., & Jerit, J. (2018). Disgust, anxiety, and political learning in the face of threat. *American Journal of Political Science*, *62* (2), 266–279.
Clifford, S., & Piston, S. (2017). Explaining public support for counterproductive homelessness policy: The role of disgust. *Political Behavior*, *39*, 503–525.
Cohen-Chen, S., Halperin, E., Crisp, R. J., & Gross, J. J. (2014). Hope in the Middle East: Malleability beliefs, hope, and the willingness to compromise for peace. *Social Psychological and Personality Science*, *5* (1), 67–75.
Erisen, C. (2018). *Political behavior and the emotional citizen*. London: Palgrave Macmillan.
Georgarakis, G. N. (2023). Yikes! The effect of incidental disgust and information on public attitudes during the COVID-19 pandemic. *Political Psychology*, *44* (3), 493–513.
Greenaway, K. H., Cichocka, A., Van Veelen, R., Likki, T., & Branscombe, N. R. (2016). Feeling hopeful inspires support for social change. *Political Psychology*, *37* (1), 89–107.
Grillon, C. (2008). Models and mechanisms of anxiety: Evidence from startle studies. *Psychopharmacology*, *199*, 421–437.
Halperin, E., Bar-Tal, D., Nets-Zehngut, R., & Drori, E. (2008). Emotions in conflict: Correlates of fear and hope in the Israeli-Jewish society. *Peace and Conflict: Journal of Peace Psychology*, *14* (3), 233–258.
Han, J., Cha, M., & Lee, W. (2020). Anger contributes to the spread of COVID-19 misinformation. *Harvard Kennedy School Misinformation Review*, *1* (3), 1–14.
Huddy, L., Feldman, S., & Cassese, E. (2007). On the distinct political effects of anxiety and anger. In G. E. Marcus, W. Russell Neuman, M. MacKuen, & A. N. Crigler (Eds.), *The affect effect: Dynamics of emotion in political thinking and behavior* (pp. 202–230). Chicago, IL: Chicago Scholarship Online.
Huddy, L., Feldman, S., Taber, C., & Lahav, G. (2005). Threat, anxiety, and support of antiterrorism policies. *American Journal of Political Science*, *49* (3), 593–608.
Kam, C. D., & Estes, B. A. (2016). Disgust sensitivity and public demand for protection. *The Journal of Politics*, *78* (2), 481–496.
Lazarus, R. S. (1991). *Emotion and adaptation*. Oxford: Oxford University Press.

Lerner, J. S., & Keltner, D. (2001). Fear, anger, and risk. *Journal of Personality and Social Psychology*, *81*, 146–159.

Leshem, O. A., & Halperin, E. (2020). Hope during conflict. In S. C. van den Heuvel (Ed.), *Historical and multidisciplinary perspectives on hope* (pp. 179–196). Cham: Springer International Publishing.

Lodge, M., McGraw, K. M., & Stroh, P. (1989). An impression-driven model of candidate evaluation. *American Political Science Review*, *83* (2), 399–419.

Lodge, M., Steenbergen, M. R., & Brau, S. (1995). The responsive voter: Campaign information and the dynamics of candidate evaluation. *American Political Science Review*, *89* (2), 309–326.

Lodge, M., & Taber, C. S. (2005). The automaticity of affect for political leaders, groups, and issues: An experimental test of the hot cognition hypothesis. *Political Psychology*, *26* (3), 455–482.

MacKuen, M., Wolak, J., Keele, L., & Marcus, G. E. (2010). Civic engagements: Resolute partisanship or reflective deliberation. *American Journal of Political Science*, *54* (2), 440–458.

Marcus, G. E. (2013). *Political psychology: Neuroscience, genetics, and politics.* Oxford: Oxford University Press.

Marcus, G. E., Neuman, W. R., & MacKuen, M. (2000). *Affective intelligence and political judgment.* Chicago: University of Chicago Press.

Marcus, G. E., Neuman, W. R., & MacKuen, M. B. (2017). Measuring emotional response: Comparing alternative approaches to measurement. *Political Science Research and Methods*, *5* (4), 733–754.

Nai, A., Schemeil, Y., & Marie, J. L. (2017). Anxiety, sophistication, and resistance to persuasion: Evidence from a quasi-experimental survey on global climate change. *Political Psychology*, *38* (1), 137–156.

Navarrete, C. D., & Fessler, D. M. (2006). Disease avoidance and ethnocentrism: The effects of disease vulnerability and disgust sensitivity on intergroup attitudes. *Evolution and Human Behavior*, *27* (4), 270–282.

Phoenix, D. L. (2019). *The anger gap: How race shapes emotion in politics.* Cambridge: Cambridge University Press.

Redlawsk, D. P. (2002). Hot cognition or cool consideration? Testing the effects of motivated reasoning on political decision making. *Journal of Politics*, *64* (4), 1021–1044.

Redlawsk, D. P., Civettini, A. J., & Emmerson, K. M. (2010). The affective tipping point: Do motivated reasoners ever "get it"? *Political Psychology*, *31* (4), 563–593.

Rhodes-Purdy, M., Navarre, R., & Utych, S. M. (2023). *The age of discontent: Populism, extremism, and conspiracy theories in contemporary democracies.* Cambridge: Cambridge University Press.

Rico, G., Guinjoan, M., & Anduiza, E. (2017). The emotional underpinnings of populism: How anger and fear affect populist attitudes. *Swiss Political Science Review*, *23* (4), 444–461.

Rozin, P., Haidt, J., & McCauley, C. R. (2016). Disgust. In M. Lewis, J. M. Haviland-Jones, & L. F. Barrett (Eds.), *Handbook of emotions* (4rd ed., pp. 815–833). Surrey: The Guilford Press.

Smith, C. A., & Ellsworth, P. C. (1985). Patterns of cognitive appraisal in emotion. *Journal of Personality and Social Psychology*, *48* (4), 813–838.

Suhay, E., & Erisen, C. (2018). The role of anger in the biased assimilation of political information. *Political Psychology*, *39* (4), 793–810.

Taber, C. S., & Lodge, M. (2006). Motivated skepticism in the evaluation of political beliefs. *American Journal of Political Science*, *50* (3), 755–769.
Valentino, N. A., Brader, T., Groenendyk, E. W., Gregorowicz, K., & Hutchings, V. L. (2011). Election night's alright for fighting: The role of emotions in political participation. *The Journal of Politics*, *73* (1), 156–170.
Valentino, N. A., Hutchings, V. L., Banks, A. J., & Davis, A. K. (2008). Is a worried citizen a good citizen? Emotions, political information seeking, and learning via the internet. *Political Psychology*, *29* (2), 247–273.
Valentino, N. A., & Neuner, F. G. (2017). Why the sky didn't fall: Mobilizing anger in reaction to voter ID laws. *Political Psychology*, *38* (2), 331–350.
Vasilopoulos, P. (2018). Terrorist events, emotional reactions, and political participation: The 2015 Paris attacks. *West European Politics*, *41* (1), 102–127.
Vasilopoulos, P., Marcus, G. E., Valentino, N. A., & Foucault, M. (2019). Fear, anger, and voting for the far right: Evidence from the November 13, 2015 Paris terror attacks. *Political Psychology*, *40* (4), 679–704.
Vasilopoulos, P., McAvay, H., Brouard, S., & Foucault, M. (2023). Emotions, governmental trust and support for the restriction of civil liberties during the covid-19 pandemic. *European Journal of Political Research*, *62* (2), 422–442.
Widmann, T. (2021). How emotional are populists really? Factors explaining emotional appeals in the communication of political parties. *Political Psychology*, *42* (1), 163–181.
Wlodarczyk, A., Basabe, N., Páez, D., & Zumeta, L. (2017). Hope and anger as mediators between collective action frames and participation in collective mobilization: The case of 15-M. *Journal of Social and Political Psychology*, *5* (1), 200–223.

Section 3

Key Methodologies

Chapter 9

Key Methodologies in Political Psychology

Introduction

Being at the intersection of psychology and political science, political psychology employs a wide range of methods to investigate the psychological substrates of political behavior and the impact of social and political arrangements on human psychology. Despite this methodological pluralism, the field of political psychology is predominantly quantitative. Around ¾ of article submissions in *Political Psychology*, which is the flagship scientific journal of the discipline, use quantitative methods, while only around a quarter draw on qualitative methods (Mintz & Mograbi, 2015). Even though quantitativists and qualitativists often perceive themselves as belonging to opposing camps, the two approaches are not necessarily in tension: They just aim to answer different questions around political psychology. **Quantitative approaches** in their various forms typically aim to measure various psychological traits or life experiences and associate them with political choices. They typically involve administering closed-ended questionnaires to large numbers of participants and analyzing the data using statistical techniques. **Qualitative approaches** on the other hand, focus on rich, detailed accounts of a small number of participants to understand themes, nuances, and motifs that mass quantitative studies may overlook. The complementarity of quantitative and qualitative approaches has spurred a recent wave of mixed methods research, or in other words, work that employs both methodological

> **Quantitative approaches**: Research methods that use numerical data typically collected through closed-type questionnaires and analyzed by statistical techniques.
>
> **Qualitative approaches**: Research methods focusing on detailed, in-depth data from a small number of participants to understand meanings, feelings, processes, and motivations underlying political behavior.

DOI: 10.4324/9781003460084-12

approaches. This chapter offers a concise overview of some of the most popular methods used in political psychology, presenting their advantages and limitations.

Quantitative Approaches in Political Psychology

Correlational Studies – The Survey Approach

Survey research involves collecting data about individuals using questionnaires or interviews. Surveys are a very common method for collecting quantitative data. Most people have completed at least one survey at some point in their lives whether in the form of a customer satisfaction survey, a university module evaluation, a patient experience, or a public opinion poll. The advantage of surveys is that they allow a researcher to obtain a wealth of information quickly (Kiess & Green, 2019). Researchers can then use this data to depict trends in the population they are interested in, such as the percentage of people who are supportive of a policy. They can also examine which factors this support is associated with and how it varies between different social groups.

In fact, one of the most commonly used methods in political psychology involves measuring a number of characteristics in a population sample and assessing, using quantitative methods, whether and how these characteristics relate to each other. For example, a political psychologist may be interested in whether specific personality traits (e.g., the extent to which we empathize with others) are related to political ideology (e.g., Bakker et al., 2016). Other examples are whether experiencing anger makes us more likely to participate in politics (e.g., Valentino et al., 2011), or whether living in ethnically diverse areas is associated with sympathy or hostility toward ethnic minorities (e.g., Green et al., 2016). All of these questions aim at exploring whether one variable is associated with another one.

To answer this type of question, the researcher first needs to consider the population they want to study (the target population). For instance, they could be interested in the link between personality and ideology in an established democracy with a market economy such as the United Kingdom. Or alternatively they could be interested in investigating this relationship in one former communist country, all former communist countries, or even at a global level (e.g., Fatke, 2017). Once the population has been identified the next task is to decide on a **sample** that will be drawn out of this population. Of course, ideally, we would like to ask every single person about their personality traits and their ideological preferences. This however would be unrealistic both in terms of practical feasibility and cost. It would also be unnecessary, as we could draw on a large and diverse sample that would allow us to generalize our findings back to the general population. To achieve such a sample, an appropriate sampling method must be used.

Sampling

Sampling methods – or the means by which a sample is drawn from the target population – are distinguished by two types: **probability-based** and **non-probability-based**. Non-probability samples are not representative of the population they intend to measure. They are typically used when a researcher seeks to collect data about a population that is "hard to survey", meaning they are hard to identify, contact, reach, or unlikely to accept to be interviewed by a researcher (Khoury, 2020; Tourangeau, 2014). Examples include members of religious cults, undocumented immigrants, or far-right activists. The challenge that a researcher faces here is that the number and properties of the population they seek to survey are unknown. Sometimes non-probability samples are used in marketing research, mostly because it is a very cost-effective way to build a sample. For instance, interviewers may recruit participants waiting outside of train stations or in shopping malls to ask their opinions about products. The problem with this method of sampling is that it is hard to have confidence that the obtained results can be in any way representative of the population one intends to survey. In our example, people who use the train to commute are more likely to be employed and urban dwellers. Researchers employing this strategy risk undersampling retirees, people with disabilities, drivers, and remote workers, who may hold different perspectives on the issue under investigation.

> **Probability-based sample**: A sample in which participants have a known probability of being selected into the sample, which facilitates the generalizability of obtained results.
>
> **Non-probability-based sample**: A sample where participants do not have a known or equal chance.

On the other hand, probability sampling "assumes that each person within a given population has a certain known chance of being included in a sample" (Glynn et al., 2004, p. 78). The purest form of probability sampling is **random sampling**, where each population member has the same chance of being selected. The aim of probability sampling is to construct a sample that is representative of the general population. In other words, "if you know the chances or odds that people in the population have of being included in the sample, you also know the chances or odds that whatever you measure in the sample also occurs in the population" (Glynn et al., 2004, p. 78).

> **Random sample**: A sample where every individual of the target population has an equal chance of being selected, increasing representativeness.

However, there is inevitably a difference between the population and the sample values, which is called **sampling error** and tends to be lower in larger samples.

> **Sampling error**: The difference between a population value and the estimated value obtained from a sample.

Many students confuse the size of the sample with its representativeness. Big samples are considered more robust and more representative compared to smaller samples. This is not necessarily true. A probability sample of 600 participants is much more representative of the United States general population compared to a non-probability sample, even if the latter consists of several million people (see Box 9.1)

Box 9.1 Sampling Size and Validity of Results: The Literary Digest

The Literary Digest was a popular US magazine that conducted large-scale polls to predict the winners of Presidential Elections since the 1920s. Their sampling method for predicting the winner of the 1936 election was to mail out 10 million ballots to potential voters. More than 2.3 million potential voters returned the ballot, which constitutes an enormous sample by any modern standards. Their poll result gave the Republican candidate, Alfred Landon, 55 per cent of the vote and the incumbent Democrat president Franklin Roosevelt 41 per cent. The actual election however ended up in a landslide victory for Roosevelt, who won comfortably gathering 61 per cent, against just 37 per cent for his opponent.

The dramatically wrong prediction was a big blow for the magazine's prestige. But what had gone so wrong? There were two key problems. One was that the list of potential voters was constructed using registries of automobile owners and telephone subscribers, who tended to come from higher incomes and were less likely to support a Democratic candidate. The other was that just one in four potential participants returned their ballot and people from higher incomes were more likely to do so.

During the same period the young statistician George Gallup conducted his own presidential poll using a much smaller sample of around 50,000 respondents. Even though his prediction was not perfect, he still correctly called Roosevelt as the winner of the election. The key to his successful prediction was that his sample was chosen using methods of random selection of participants, increasing its representativeness compared to the flawed sample of the Literary Digest poll. The 1936 election established Gallup as a pioneer in the emerging field of scientific polling and dealt an irreversible blow to the prestige of Literary Digest.

Cross-sectional v. Panel Surveys

Most surveys concern the measurement of specific traits and behaviors of a population at one point in time. These surveys are called **cross-sectional**, that is, a one-off measurement of the characteristics of the sample of a population. Cross-sectional studies are useful for understanding differences between groups. For example, using a one-off survey we can investigate whether people who feel angry over their financial situation are more likely to vote for populist parties compared to people who do not feel angry.

> **Cross-sectional survey**: A survey that is carried out at a single specific point in time.
>
> **Panel survey**: A survey design in which the same participants are surveyed repeatedly over time.

An alternative survey method is to ask the same sample of people the same questions over time. This is called a **panel survey**. This method allows a researcher to observe *within* person change or in other words how changes in one's circumstances relate to changes in other traits or behaviors. A panel study allows us to compare the same people in two or more time points. For example, it allows us to assess whether *becoming* angry over one's financial situation makes one become more likely to vote for populist parties, compared to when they were not feeling angry. The use of panel data is particularly important as it allows us to better estimate causal relationships as opposed to mere correlations between variables. A drawback of this method is that it is particularly time-consuming and expensive. Another issue is that some people who have been contacted the first time may not be available or willing to fill in the survey a second time. This is called panel attrition and can be an important source of bias in the obtained results. It is problematic because people who choose to opt out of the study may have specific demographic and psychological characteristics that correlate with the outcome of interest, hence introducing bias and undermining the research findings.

Experiments

Experiments are one of the most commonly used and robust methods in political psychology. Experiments help us better understand causal effects in political psychological processes. Ideally, to understand whether an effect is causal or not we would need to observe the same person under a condition where an intervention is not administered and in one where the intervention is administered. The key characteristic of experiments is that the researcher creates the conditions of investigation rather than being an observer in the process as is the case with research surveys. This is achieved by randomly assigning individuals to different groups. One is typically called the **control group**, which is the group that does not receive any intervention. The second is the **treatment group**, which is the group that receives the intervention. The **random assignment** means that each of the participants in the experiment has the same chance of ending up in the control or the treatment group. By allocating respondents to groups randomly the experimenter ends up having two groups with similar demographic or attitudinal characteristics. The researchers then administer an intervention to the treatment group and compare the behavior of the treatment group to the control group. Because the two groups are similar in everything *except* the intervention, the researcher can conclude with confidence whether the intervention had an effect. In other words, the researcher is confident that the group that did not receive the treatment would have behaved in the same way as the treatment group if they had received the treatment.

Experiment: A research design where the investigator randomly assigns participants to a control group and to one or more treatment groups in order to isolate the causal effect of an intervention.

Control group: The group in an experiment that does not receive an intervention and serves as a baseline group.

Treatment group: The group in an experiment that receives the intervention whose effect is being evaluated.

Random assignment (in experiments): The process of allocating participants to control and treatment groups by chance, ensuring the creation of two groups with similar characteristics prior to an experimental intervention.

A frequently mentioned example comes from political campaigning. There is much speculation on whether political debates that take place in many countries between candidates before an election make any difference to the electoral outcome or not. This question can be answered in several ways. One way would be to design a survey during an election campaign – with the method that we described above – and ask a representative sample of voters whether they happened to watch the debate or not. One could then compare the vote intentions between those who did and did not watch the debate. However, it would be very hard to convince the scientific community that the obtained results really show whether the debate mattered or not as there is a key problem: People chose themselves whether to watch the debate or not, and people who like to watch political debates may differ from the ones who do not. For one, in many countries older people are more interested in politics, more likely to watch television, and more likely to vote for conservative parties compared to younger generations. This means that the obtained results may simply reflect differences between those who like watching debates on TV and those who do not and the debate by itself may not have played any role in their voting intention. Even if a researcher considers differences in age or other characteristics, they will never be able to control for every single characteristic.

An alternative way would be to use an experiment. In this case the researcher would recruit a sample of voters. Then, by flipping a coin, the researcher would randomly allocate each respondent to one of two groups. The first group (control group) would watch an unrelated TV program (or even not watch TV at all). The second, which is the treatment group, would watch the debate. Then, the researcher would invite both groups to answer questions on their voting intentions. Because both groups have been allocated at random the researcher can safely assume that any difference in their vote intention can only have been caused by watching the debate.

Despite their tremendous potential for identifying causal effects, experimentalists need to be cautious about a few potential issues. First, they need to ensure that the experiment has **internal validity** or the criterion that "experimental procedures must measure the concepts they are intended to measure" (Glynn et al., 2004, p. 104). In other words, researchers need to be certain that it was their treatment that caused the effect and not an external factor that unintentionally came with the treatment. For example, if during the debate interval there were candidate advertisements (as often is the case in real life) then it could have been the ads rather than the debate that swayed the treatment group. Similarly, if the control group watched a television program that may have touched on a political issue then this could have well interfered with the obtained results. Ensuring internal validity is much more difficult than it sounds.

A second concern is **external validity** or – in our example – the extent to which the obtained findings from the sample of voters that we chose to watch the debate can be generalized to the broader population. Recruiting large and diverse samples for experiments is very expensive. Most of the time researchers rely on convenience samples or even university students. People who agree to participate in these types of experiments are more likely to be interested in politics and thus atypically attentive to political debates, whereas average voters would not pay so much attention. Another issue concerning external validity is the extent to which the experimental setting reflects real-world conditions. For example, perhaps when

Internal validity: The extent to which an experimental effect is truly caused by the treatment and not by other confounding factors or errors in the study design.

External validity: The extent to which research findings can be generalized beyond the specific sample, context, and setting that a study was conducted in.

people are called to participate in a scientific study, they will pay more attention to the content that is shown to them compared to what they would do in their everyday life.

Lab Experiments

Experiments can take place in laboratories. Participants are invited by a researcher to a lab to perform tasks or answer questions after having been randomly allocated to different groups. The key advantage of **lab experiments** is that the experimenter can fully control the setting and the conditions under which the experiment takes place (Falk & Heckman, 2009). For instance, the researcher can fully control the information participants are exposed to before reaching a decision, which increases internal validity because the experimenter can be confident that it is their treatment that affected the outcome rather than some external factor. Participants in these experiments are convenience samples who are typically given a small fee to participate in the study. Many times, the sample consists of undergraduate students who agree to participate for extra class credit. Some argue that the lack of a representative sample is not necessarily a drawback as some research questions do not make assumptions over the composition of participants, in other words they predict that the effect should be observed across groups. Others posit that the homogeneity of samples consisting of students, for example, in terms of age, education, and political interest pose a drawback for external validity, depending on the hypothesis (see Druckman & Kam, 2011 for a discussion). The important issue is that the control and treatment groups are balanced in demographic and attitudinal characteristics, which is achieved by the random assignment. Some critics argue that laboratory experiments lack realism, which poses barriers to external validity. Hence researchers often try to make the lab seem as realistic as possible.

Lab experiments: Experiments conducted in a laboratory setting where experimentalists can maximize control over the environment.

Box 9.2 Lab Experiment Example – Does Anxiety Make Us More Likely to Seek Out Political Information?

An example of an interesting lab experiment comes from Valentino et al. (2008). The researchers were interested in testing whether different negative emotions increase or decrease political information seeking, learning, and political attention. To find out, they recruited participants using flyers at local businesses and the university area of their town. Subjects were told they would receive 10$ to answer questions "about media habits and current events". After completing a first, pre-test questionnaire the participants were randomly allocated to one of a total of four groups. The researchers made sure that the groups were balanced in terms of sociodemographic and partisan variables or, in other words, confirmed that the random allocation was successful. The respondents then sat in front of a computer screen. They were asked to "describe something during the current [US 2004 Presidential Election] campaign that made them feel" the emotion in question: "angry" for the respondents of group 1, afraid (group 2), or enthusiastic (group 3). A final group was asked to describe something that made them feel relaxed. This was the control group. The goal of the experimenters was to compare the political attention, learning, and information processing of those in the control group compared to those in each of the other three groups. Then respondents were provided with the opportunity to visit the websites of the presidential candidates and learn about their policies. The websites were designed to replicate the official websites of the major candidates. Valentino et al. then compared how much time respondents of each of the groups spent on these websites. They found that those in the anxiety group were more likely to seek out information about the candidates. Because respondents were allocated randomly in these four groups the researchers were confident that it was anxiety that had *caused* the differences in attention and not some other pre-existing factor.

Field Experiments

The aim of **field experiments** is to maintain the internal validity of laboratory experiments but at the same time maximize external validity, the generalizability of obtained findings. Unlike laboratory experiments, field experiments take place in real-world contexts. They "attempt to assess the effects of an intervention under naturalistic conditions" (Green, 2022, p. 56) and typically involve massive samples. In field experiments, participants are usually unaware that they are taking part in a study. Typically, the procedure works as follows (Green, 2022). Using random allocation, researchers assign a number of household addresses in a given area (e.g., a small town or suburb) to the treatment group and others to the control group. Researchers visit both the treatment and the control groups: The treatment group is exposed to an intervention (e.g., a brief discussion aiming at motivating them to turn out to vote), while the control group is exposed

Field experiments: Experiments conducted in real-world settings and combine random assignment with naturalistic conditions.

to an unrelated message (e.g., over the benefits of recycling). The researchers then compare differences in the political behavior (e.g., actual turnout) of the two groups, sometimes using administrative data, without the participants having ever been aware that they participated in a study (Green, 2022).

Field experiments are often used to assess the effects of political campaigns. For example, field experiments in political psychology seek to use psychological theories to increase electoral registration and turnout, especially among marginalized groups (e.g., Braconnier et al., 2017). Other experimentalists are occupied with questions of intergroup relations and effective interventions to reduce prejudice in various settings (e.g., Broockman & Kalla, 2016; Kalla & Broockman, 2020; Larson & Lewis, 2025).

Box 9.3 Can Canvassing Durably Reduce Transphobia? A Field Experiment

Broockman and Kalla (2016) conducted a field experiment to assess the impact of perspective-taking on attitudes toward transgender people in the US. Perspective-taking involves a short conversation that invites the participant to take the perspective of an outgroup and has been shown to increase empathy and reduce prejudice. The experiment was administered as follows. First, the research team recruited a sample of registered voters in Miami, Florida, and sent them a baseline survey that included several questions about politics, including a few items on transgender issues. Then, they randomly assigned them to either a treatment group that was exposed to the perspective-taking treatment or a control group that was targeted with a conversation about recycling. 56 canvassers would knock on each respondent's door and invite them to engage in conversation about either transgender people or recycling depending on the group to which the respondents were assigned. In the treatment group, the canvasser asked the participants to "talk about a time that they themselves were judged negatively for being different" and then consider "how their own experience offered a window into transgender people's experiences" (Broockman & Kalla, 2016, p. 221). Finally, after the intervention both the control and treatment groups were again sent a survey to measure political attitudes, including the same items on transgender issues. The goal was to assess whether perspective-taking was an efficient way to reduce transphobia by comparing the control and treatment groups. Their results showed that it was. Before the intervention, both control and treatment group participants had similar attitudes toward transgender people. Yet after the intervention, participants in the treatment group (i.e., those who participated in the perspective-taking conversation) were significantly more accepting of transgender people compared to the control group (those who engaged in a conversation about recycling). Interestingly, the differences in attitudes between the two groups lasted for several months.

Natural Experiments

Natural experiments: Studies that take advantage of real-world events or situations that affect some people and not others in ways that approximate random assignment, hence allowing for the assessment of causal effects.

A final type of experiment concerns **natural experiments**. Here, an event takes place in the real world that creates the conditions for an experiment by randomly affecting some people and not others. In other words in natural experiments "nature acts in a way that is close to how a researcher, given the choice, would have intervened" (Morton & Williams, 2008, p. 343). Examples of natural experiments include the study of different types of unexpected events such as terror attacks or natural disasters on social and political attitudes (e.g., Visconti, 2022).

Qualitative Methods

Qualitative studies offer an alternative set of methodological tools to conduct political psychology research. Qualitative data come with the important advantage of offering rich and detailed insights into the motivations that guide human behavior. They allow for an investigation of the process of political attitude formation and the thought processes that people use to reach political conclusions. In ethnographic research, for instance, the researcher interacts with study participants by spending time with them in their social environment and becoming a participant in their daily lives. This allows for a fuller understanding of individuals' psychological motivations and political decision-making processes. In contrast with quantitative research where the interest is in the association of two or more variables, in qualitative research the focus is on the individual perspectives that lead to political decision-making.

Interviews

Qualitative researchers often rely on **in-depth interviews** for collecting data. The purpose of in-depth interviews is to gather a detailed account of the participant's views of a research topic that includes a deep understanding of their perception, emotion, meaning, and knowledge (Yates, 2003). In-depth interviews may be unstructured (resembling more of a conversation with the participant), structured (standardized across participants), or semi-structured. In all cases, in qualitative research, researchers focus on the "speaker's perspective" and are committed to "understanding events, actions, values etc., from the perspective of the person being studied" as an attempt to "see through the eyes of the person being studied" (Yates, 2003, p. 157). In-depth interviews are common in political psychology research having been used for investigating a diverse set of research questions. For instance, Moss and Sandbakken interviewed 16 individuals in depth during the first phase of the Covid-19 pandemic in Norway to understand the psychological mechanisms behind compliance with liberty-restricting measures and the ways in which government narratives over the pandemic become internalized and accepted (2021). Another example comes from Zisakou et al. (2024) who interviewed 25 refugees in two major Greek cities to explore how interactions with natives and other refugees in a common urban space cultivate opportunities for political expression and participation.

In-depth interviews: A qualitative research method involving detailed unstructured or structured conversations with participants to gain insights into their perspectives, emotions, and experiences regarding a research topic.

Focus Groups

Focus groups involve a relaxed and informal discussion on a specific topic between a small number of selected individuals (usually four to ten) guided by a moderator. The groups may be homogeneous based on characteristics such as gender, age, ethnic background, or political beliefs. The focus group aims not only at revealing participants' individual perceptions, narratives, and psychological motifs; the researcher also observes how these are expressed through interaction and conversation among the members of a group. Sometimes this can be a drawback. For instance, there is always the risk that some members of the focus group dominate the conversation offering little space for the expression of all viewpoints (Smithson, 2000). Further, the presence of a moderator makes these discussions less natural than those which would occur in the real world. That said, focus groups constitute a very useful tool for political psychologists. Studies based on focus

Focus groups: A qualitative research method involving guided discussions among a small group of participants.

group methodology have investigated a diverse and rich set of themes across different settings: For example, Nair and Vollhardt used focus groups to investigate how low-status groups in India experience and understand disadvantage and stigmatization (2019); Atikcan and Hand studied how individual differences in moral foundations affected vote choice in the 2018 Irish referendum on abortion (2024); Howarth and Andreouli used pupil and teacher focus groups to explore how diversity is perceived and experienced in schools in England (2016).

Ethnography

Ethnography: A qualitative method in which the researcher observes, participates, and engages in the everyday interactions of the population under study.

Unlike focus groups that take place in a controlled environment, **ethnography** entails "immersion in the place and lives of people under study" (Wedeen, 2010, p. 257). In most ethnographic research, the researcher is a participant observer. They spend time in a community of people, developing relationships, observing, and engaging in everyday activity. This may include having informal conversations or attending public gatherings, protests, and other political events. The aim of the ethnographer is not merely to simply transcribe conversations with their subjects but to "understand the world as their subjects see it" or in other words to provide a "detailed account of the lives of respondents, in order to make it possible for an outsider to comprehend the meanings and motivations associated with their experiences" (Perez, 2024, p. 216). Initially conceived and developed as a methodological tool in social anthropology that allowed researchers to study the cultural practices of local populations, ethnography has become a particularly useful tool among political psychologists. It allows for rich psychological accounts of people's political behaviors and social identity development particularly in the context of their local environment (e.g., Hochschild, 2016; Ropert & Di Masso, 2021).

The seminal study of Cramer (2012), for instance, used ethnographic methods to investigate why low-income people support policies and candidates that seemingly go against their self-interest. She attended informal meetings held by voluntary groups in casual settings such as restaurants or gas stations across the US state of Wisconsin. Cramer found that a recurring theme in political discussions was rural consciousness: People developed a distinct social identity based on their rural background, positioning themselves in opposition to the urban residents of the same state. They attributed their communities' deprivation to the urban political elites and favored policies aiming at curtailing their influence. Consequently, they stood against big government. In Cramer's words "their reluctance to tax the rich is rooted in a complex narrative in which government action is by definition an injustice to themselves" (p. 529).

In her own ethnographic study, Alice Hochschild asks a similar question: Why do people of some of the poorest states in the United States endorse policies that have a direct detrimental economic and environmental impact in their own local communities? To answer what she calls this 'Great Paradox' she spent five years in Louisiana following 40 Tea Party supporters. Her work reveals strong emotional underpinnings of far-right support in the United States, including anxiety and particularly anger stemming from a sense of loss of honor. Discussions and interviews with participants revealed that these emotions are cultivated by the perception that immigrants, minorities, and other groups are "cutting the line" ahead of hardworking Americans through federal programs. Hence, turning to ultraconservative, populist candidates such as Trump is an angry reaction to their sense of "betrayal" by the federal government.

Research Ethics and Reproducibility

Political psychology typically involves research with human subjects. Consequently, as in any other research field that involves people, researchers must respect a set of ethical rules that ensures that research is conducted responsibly in a way that does not entail harm for participants. The British Psychological Society lists four ethical principles or sets of values that psychologists, including political psychologists should abide by: Respect for the dignity of persons (e.g., acquiring consent; considering the impact on well-being and the broader social environment; showing empathy and compassion with participants); Competence (acquisition of appropriate skills; awareness of one's limits of expertise); responsibility (e.g., professional accountability) and integrity (e.g., honesty, fairness, and avoidance of exploitation and conflict of interest).

During the 2010s psychology went through a "replication crisis" when researchers discovered that many findings of past seminal studies could not be reproduced. It soon became apparent that some of these failures were due to questionable research practices. This was partly attributed to the pressure that many researchers feel to continuously publish novel research findings to advance their academic careers. The replication crisis undermined confidence in the discipline. At the same time, it spurred a large wave of reforms and initiatives aimed at ensuring that published psychological research is robust, valid, and trustworthy. Such initiatives, often described under the umbrella term **Open Science**, included for instance the development of large-scale collaborations

> **Open science**: A group of research practices aiming at increasing the credibility of obtained research findings by initiatives such as data sharing between researchers, preregistration of theoretical expectations, and open access to research materials.

with the aim of systematically replicating past work. Further, many journals now require authors to upload their data and analysis code so that they can be easily reproduced by any interested party. Another increasingly popular practice is the preregistration of theoretical expectations before the data have been analyzed, so as to ensure that researchers will not try to tailor their theory to fit their obtained results.

Conclusion

This chapter provided an overview of some of the most common methods used in political psychological research. The list of methodological approaches in an interdisciplinary field such as political psychology is of course much longer than the methodological approaches we discussed. It also extends to discourse and content analysis, social network analysis, or neuroimaging. The choice of method predominantly depends on the type of question the researcher wants to ask and the theoretical framework they intend to follow. Method choice is not necessarily an either/or decision. Increasingly, leading political psychology research (and social science research more broadly) relies on more than one method. These mixed methods designs combine the richness and detail of qualitative analyses with the representativeness and causal leverage of quantitative studies.

Further Reading

Druckman, J. N., Green, D. P., Kuklinski, J., & Lupia, A. (Eds.). *Cambridge handbook of experimental political science*. New York: Cambridge. A detailed guide on the theory and practice of experiments in political science.

Nosek, B. A., Hardwicke, T. E., Moshontz, H., Allard, A., Corker, K. S., Dreber, A., … & Vazire, S. (2022). Replicability, robustness, and reproducibility in psychological science. *Annual Review of Psychology*, *73* (1), 719–748. A thorough review of issues of replicability, robustness, and reproducibility in psychology research.

References

Atikcan, E. Ö., & Hand, K. (2024). Moral framing and referendum politics: Navigating the empathy battlefield. *Political Psychology*, *45* (1), 193–210.

Bakker, B. N., Rooduijn, M., & Schumacher, G. (2016). The psychological roots of populist voting: Evidence from the United States, the Netherlands and Germany. *European Journal of Political Research*, *55* (2), 302–320.

Braconnier, C., Dormagen, J. Y., & Pons, V. (2017). Voter registration costs and disenfranchisement: experimental evidence from France. *American Political Science Review*, *111* (3), 584–604.

Broockman, D., & Kalla, J. (2016). Durably reducing transphobia: A field experiment on door-to-door canvassing. *Science*, *352* (6282), 220–224.

Cramer, K. W. (2012). Putting inequality in its place: Rural consciousness and the power of perspective. *American Political Science Review*, *106* (3), 517–532.

Druckman, J. N., & Kam, C. D. (2011). Students as experimental participants. In J. N. Druckman, D. P. Greene, & J. H. Kuklinski (Eds.), *Cambridge handbook of experimental political science* (pp. 41–57). Cambridge: Cambridge University Press.

Falk, A., & Heckman, J. J. (2009). Lab experiments are a major source of knowledge in the social sciences. *Science, 326* (5952), 535–538.

Fatke, M. (2017). Personality traits and political ideology: A first global assessment. *Political Psychology, 38* (5), 881–899.

Green, D. P. (2022). *Social science experiments: A hands-on introduction.* Cambridge: Cambridge University Press.

Green, E. G., Sarrasin, O., Baur, R., & Fasel, N. (2016). From stigmatized immigrants to radical right voting: A multilevel study on the role of threat and contact. *Political Psychology, 37* (4), 465–480.

Glynn, C.J, Herbst, S., O'Keefe, G. J., Shapiro, R. Y. & M. Lindeman. (2004). *Public opinion* (2nd ed.). Boulder, CO: Westview Press.

Hochschild, A. R. (2016). *Strangers in their own land: Anger and mourning on the American right.* New York: The New Press.

Howarth, C., & Andreouli, E. (2016). "Nobody wants to be an outsider": From diversity management to diversity engagement. *Political Psychology, 37* (3), 327–340.

Kalla, J. L., & Broockman, D. E. (2020). Reducing exclusionary attitudes through interpersonal conversation: Evidence from three field experiments. *American Political Science Review, 114* (2), 410–425.

Khoury, R. B. (2020). Hard-to-survey populations and respondent-driven sampling: Expanding the political science toolbox. *Perspectives on Politics, 18* (2), 509–526.

Kiess, H. O., & Green, B. A. (2019). *Statistical concepts for the behavioral sciences.* Cambridge: Cambridge University Press.

Larson, J. M., & Lewis, J. I. (2025). Reducing prejudice towards refugees in Uganda: Evidence that social networks influence attitude change. *American Political Science Review, 119* (1), 349–367.

Mintz, A., & Mograbi, E. (2015). Political psychology: Submissions, acceptances, downloads, and citations. *Political Psychology, 36* (3), 267–275.

Morton, R. B., & Williams, K. C. (2008). Experimentation in political science. In J. M. Box-Steffensmeier, H. E. Brady, & D. Collier (Eds.), *The Oxford handbook of political methodology.* Oxford: Oxford University Press (pp. 339–356).

Moss, S. M., & Sandbakken, E. M. (2021). "Everybody needs to do their part, so we can get this under control." Reactions to the Norwegian government meta-narratives on COVID-19 measures. *Political Psychology, 42* (5), 881–898.

Nair, R., & Vollhardt, J. R. (2019). Intersectional consciousness in collective victim beliefs: Perceived intragroup differences among disadvantaged groups. *Political Psychology, 40* (5), 917–934.

Perez, M. (2024). Ethnography. In Y. Stavanakis & G. Katsambekis (Eds.), *Elgar research handbook on populism.* London: Edward Elgar Publishing (pp. 216–225).

Ropert, T., & Di Masso, A. (2021). Living there, leaving there: Identity, sociospatial mobility, and exclusion in "stigmatized neighborhoods". *Political Psychology, 42* (1), 53–69.

Smithson, J. (2000). Using and analysing focus groups: limitations and possibilities. *International Journal of Social Research Methodology, 3* (2), 103–119.

Tourangeau, R. (2014). Defining hard-to-survey populations. In R. Tourangeau, B. Edwards, T. P. Johnson, K. M. Wolter, & N. Bates (Eds.), *Hard-to-survey populations* (pp. 3–20). Cambridge: Cambridge University Press.

Valentino, N. A., Brader, T., Groenendyk, E. W., Gregorowicz, K., & Hutchings, V. L. (2011). Election night's alright for fighting: The role of emotions in political participation. *The Journal of Politics, 73* (1), 156–170.
Valentino, N. A., Hutchings, V. L., Banks, A. J., & Davis, A. K. (2008). Is a worried citizen a good citizen? Emotions, political information seeking, and learning via the internet. *Political Psychology, 29* (2), 247–273.
Visconti, G. (2022). After the flood: Disasters, ideological voting and electoral choices in Chile. *Political Behavior, 44* (4), 1985–2004.
Wedeen, L. (2010). Reflections on ethnographic work in political science. *Annual Review of Political Science, 13* (1), 255–272.
Yates, S. (2003). *Doing social science research.* London: Sage.
Zisakou, A., Figgou, L., & Andreouli, E. (2024). Integration and urban citizenship: A social-psychological approach to refugee integration through active constructions of place attachment to the city. *Political Psychology, 45* (2), 215–233.

Section 4

Key Impacts

Chapter 10

Using Political Psychology to Understand Contemporary Political Challenges and Improve Policy-Making

Introduction

Up until now this book has explored how psychological science can help us understand citizens' political behavior. This chapter focuses on practical applications of political psychology and its capacity to help address real-world social and political challenges and inform policy-making. First, it discusses applications in tackling misinformation, reducing prejudice, and outpartisan hostility, and increasing political participation. Then it provides an overview of how governments have used some of the major theories we covered in this book to increase efficiency and performance.

Using Political Psychology to Tackle Misinformation

Misinformation poses one of the biggest societal challenges of our time. It poses significant risks for public health, democracy, and intergroup relations. Misinformation has been directly linked with a broad array of deleterious societal outcomes: Vaccine and climate skepticism, distrust in the integrity of elections, radicalization, and political violence are only a few examples (e.g., Badrinathan et al., 2025; Loomba et al., 2021). Even though misinformation is not a new societal challenge, its impact is now felt more than ever. The 2020 Delhi riots targeting Muslims, the January 6th attack on the US capitol, and the Summer 2024 UK riots, are examples of how misinformation can fuel political and intergroup violence. On the other hand, the recent global Covid pandemic and the 2025 measles outbreak in Texas underline the dangers of misinformation for public health.

Effectively countering misinformation is a challenging task. The initial encounter with a piece of misinformation leaves a lasting impression in memory that persists and affects behavior even after people become aware that the information they were presented with is false (see Lewandowsky, 2021 & Lewandowsky & van der Linden, 2021 for a review). For example, research shows that fact-checking misinformation spread by political candidates does not affect attitudes toward these candidates (Nyhan et al., 2020).

In the light of these pessimistic findings, how can societies defend themselves against the deleterious effects of misinformation? In a series of studies Van den

DOI: 10.4324/9781003460084-14

Linden and colleagues designed practical interventions to address this problem (Lewandowsky & van der Linden, 2021; van der Linden et al., 2017). To this end they relied on the premises of **inoculation theory** (McGuire, 1961, 1964). Inoculation theory posits that people can develop resistance to persuasion by being exposed to a weaker version of a persuasive argument, in a similar way that vaccines protect against disease by training the immune system with a weakened version of a virus. Inoculation involves two steps. The first involves "being made aware that a persuasive attack is imminent, such as by forewarning them that political actors may want to mislead audiences' attitudes on issues such as climate change or new energy technologies" (Traberg et al., 2022, p. 138). This warning activates a perception of threat, motivating people to preserve their pre-existing beliefs. The second step involves the exposure to a "weakened (micro)dose of misinformation that contains a preemptive refutation (or prebunk) of the anticipated misleading arguments or persuasion techniques" (Roozenbeek et al., 2022, p. 1).

Inoculation theory: The hypothesis that resistance to misinformation can be built by warning people about persuasion and exposing them to weakened versions of false arguments.

Studies have found that inoculation is effective in mitigating the negative effects of misinformation, such as protecting scientifically accurate beliefs about climate change in the light of real-world misinformation (Van der Linden et al., 2017). An interesting practical application concerns the development of *Bad News* (Figure 10.1), a video game that applies the insights of

Figure 10.1 The welcome screen of *Bad News*.

inoculation theory to increase players' resistance to misinformation. The game invites players to become "disinformation and fake news tycoons" by increasing their number of followers. It draws on common real-world strategies that are used to disseminate false information. Players earn badges and win levels with each successful manipulation technique (e.g., impersonating someone else, evoking emotion, trolling). By playing the game, users are exposed to weakened versions of some of the most common forms of misinformation and become familiar with the tactics most commonly used to disperse them. Studies have found that this makes them more likely to recognize and resist misinformation, in line with the predictions of inoculation theory (Roozenbeek & Van der Linden, 2019).

Using Political Psychology to Reduce Prejudice against Low-Status Groups

International migration levels have increased significantly across the world in the last decades. The settlement of newcomers in host communities often evokes negative reactions from natives, with migrants and refugees frequently becoming targets of discrimination and prejudice. As discussed earlier in this book, the study of prejudice has been a key focus of political psychology research since the field's conceptual birth. Importantly, political psychologists are not only concerned with explaining the psychological motivations of prejudice but in some cases they also identify ways to reduce it. One key mechanism concerns **perspective-taking**. This is a psychological intervention designed to maximize empathy with an outgroup member by inviting native or majority participants to take the perspective of a member of a stigmatized group. Typically, these interventions draw on field experiments (see Chapter 9) or, in other words, large-scale interventions where researchers randomly allocate some participants to a treatment group that is encouraged to take the perspective of an outgroup member and a control group that receives no such intervention. The fact that the control and treatment groups have been allocated at random helps researchers assess the net effect of perspective-taking in reducing prejudice. Perspective-taking has been particularly successful in durably reducing hostility toward different outgroups including trans people, immigrants, or refugees (e.g., Adida et al., 2018; Broockman & Kalla, 2016 – see also Box 10.1).

> **Perspective-taking**: An intervention that aims at cultivating empathy with a member of a stigmatized group by encouraging people to take their perspective.

Box 10.1 Using Perspective-Taking to Reduce Prejudice toward Refugees in Uganda (Larson & Lewis, 2025)

Uganda hosts around one million refugees, which is the third highest refugee population worldwide. The researchers conducted experiments in four refugee-dense villages in the West Nile region of the country. Each village had between 100 and 150 households. Their aim was to shift natives' views toward refugees through perspective-taking. The intervention unfolded as follows. The researchers conducted a survey of every household in these villages with the aim of measuring people's initial attitudes toward refugees, their household characteristics, as well as a list of people they frequently interact socially with. Following this initial survey they randomly chose 50 per cent of households for their intervention. In a non-judgmental conversation, they presented people from this group with a story of a single South Sudanese refugee and her perspective, letting participants know that this person is one of the refugees residing in Uganda.

When the researchers measured attitudes toward refugees again, they found that this simple perspective-taking intervention was effective in reducing prejudice toward refugees. Importantly, participants who were invited to take the perspective of a refugee were likely to discuss issues around refugees with their friends, relatives, and neighbors in the village. This led to indirect prejudice reduction, as people who were not themselves exposed to the intervention ended up updating their preferences toward refugees in a positive way as a result of discussing with people who participated in the intervention. The research team asked their opinions again after two to three weeks and found that the effect of the intervention had persisted.

Using Political Psychology to Reduce Outpartisan Hostility and Anti-democratic Attitudes

Democracy is increasingly under threat across countries. The V-Dem institute's report for the state of democracy in 2025 is grim: "The global democratic decline deepens, regardless of how we slice the data and whichever measure we use" (Nord et al., 2025, p. 10). Putting this decline into context the report also concludes that "2024 marks the first time since 2002 when there are more autocracies than democracies in the world. This is a stark reminder of how far the democratic decline has gone" (p. 12). Democratic backsliding manifests in multiple ways (e.g., Levitsky & Ziblatt, 2019), including the weakening of democratic norms, decline in media freedom, unfounded accusations over electoral integrity, rise of political violence, and the strategic use of institutions for partisan gains. At the same time outpartisan hostility is growing in several democracies, with citizens becoming increasingly intolerant toward those with whom they disagree politically (e.g., Bergman & Fernández, 2024; Wagner, 2024).

A recent large-scale study authored by more than 75 prominent political psychologists tested the influence of 25 treatments in reducing anti-democratic attitudes and outpartisan hostility in the United States, a country which is rapidly autocratizing under Donald Trump (Voelkel et al., 2024). The authors invited ideas from social scientists, activists, and practitioners on ways to tackle the proliferation of anti-democratic ideas and partisan hostility. Some of the 25 treatments were based on theories of intergroup conflict resolution discussed in Chapter 6. For example, some were aimed at reminding study participants of their common American national identity or the joint economic interests between Democrats and Republicans. Others intended to increase their democratic system justification by reminding participants of the fundamental democratic principles that the United States is built on, while another intervention aimed at correcting stereotypes of outpartisans. The researchers found that the majority of their 25 interventions were effective in significantly reducing outpartisan hostility, while some – such as the breaking of outparty stereotypes – were also effective in reducing support for undemocratic practices. However, while the effect of these interventions lasted for more than two weeks in the case of outpartisan animosity, their effect on democratic attitudes was shorter-lived.

Using Political Psychology for Increasing Political Participation

Electoral participation is a key indicator of democratic robustness and effective citizen representation. The reasons behind electoral abstention are diverse, being rooted in numerous sociological and psychological factors (see Blais, 2006). Insights from political psychology can translate into practical interventions for increasing electoral participation, both in terms of registration and turnout. For instance, several programs aiming at increasing electoral participation draw on research on conformity and social norms that we covered in Chapter 5. There, we discussed how people have a psychological motivation to conform to the opinions and behaviors of those around them. This simple observation, based on classic studies around the development and power of social norms to guide behavior (e.g., Asch, 1951), can go a long way when it comes to mobilizing people to participate in politics.

For example, an effective method to increase electoral turnout is to inform targeted voters that most members of their community, or in some cases their direct neighbors are planning to vote. This method is well established in research (e.g., Gerber & Rogers, 2009) and has been used successfully in electoral campaigns. In fact, the Obama campaign used this form of mobilization in the 2012 US presidential election where canvassers were instructed to inform people of their neighbors' intentions to participate. Similar effects have been observed with impersonal forms of communication. For instance, a large study on Facebook tested the effectiveness of different types of political mobilization methods ahead of the 2010 US congressional elections (Bond et al., 2012). The sample was the whole American adult population who accessed Facebook on the day of the election – a total of 61 million participants. The researchers presented a group of participants with different messages at the top of their news feed. Some respondents simply viewed information about the election. Others were shown the total number of Facebook users as well as the profile pictures of six Facebook friends that reported that they had voted. The results indicated that while mere information fell short of exerting an impact, the intervention that showed that one's friends and community voted boosted turnout in the election.

Using Political Psychology for Improving Government Efficiency

The Behavioral Insights Team (BIT), sometimes referred to as the "nudge unit", was established in 2010 by the UK government. It was the first government institution to apply psychological insights to policy-making. Its mission was to boost government effectiveness and social well-being by employing psychological science. The idea was that governments could improve all sorts of policy outcomes through simple interventions instead of changes in law or governmental programs that were deemed more costly. The team's purpose was to discover ways by which citizens could be encouraged or "nudged" to behave in ways that were deemed beneficial to themselves and those around them. Even though BIT is now independent from the UK government it remains active in a broad series of social and policy domains that include policy compliance, public health outcomes, and broader societal challenges.

Typically, the team draws on insights from theories in social psychology and behavioral economics and tests their effectiveness using large-scale experiments (see Chapter 9). Throughout the years the BIT has applied insights from some of the key theories we covered in this volume. For example, one of the most successful interventions drew on social norms (see Chapter 5) to encourage the timely payment of taxes in the UK (Hallsworth et al., 2017). Using a field experiment the researchers tested different forms of a letter reminding taxpayers of their obligation to pay their taxes on time to avoid being fined. Some versions of the letter included prompts aimed at increasing social pressure to conform to the norm of paying taxes on time, by informing recipients for instance that "the great majority of people in your local area pay their tax on time" or that "most people with a debt like yours have paid it by now". Adding these simple prompts in the reminder letters significantly increased tax payment rates. The intervention was so successful that it was replicated in other countries, including the United States, Australia, and Guatemala. Another example of BIT intervention based on theories covered in this book includes increasing compliance with the health measures during the Covid-19 pandemic drawing on theories of emotion and specifically disgust to incentivize the public to wash their hands regularly. Even though the ethics (e.g., Goodwin, 2012) and the effectiveness of some of its interventions have been questioned (e.g., Sanders et al., 2021) the "nudging" model has been exported in other countries including the United States, Australia, Israel, Guatemala, and Indonesia.

Conclusion

Political psychology has important practical applications in a diverse set of policies and outcomes. In this chapter we covered citizen inoculation against misinformation, the cultivation of empathy with low-status outgroups, the bridging of partisan divisions, increasing turnout, and useful tools for governance through nudging interventions. The list does not end there. Other practical applications include interventions to countering violence against women (e.g., Green et al., 2020), increasing the persuasiveness of climate change messages (e.g., Voelkel et al., 2026), designing fairer election ballots (e.g., Miller & Krosnick, 1998), or countering radicalization and extremism (e.g., Wolfowicz et al., 2022). These interventions have very different aims and domains. What they have in common is that they are based on solid theoretical grounds and rigorous empirical methods. As political psychology evolves as a scientific field, so will the benefits it can bring for improving collective life.

Further Reading

https://inoculation.science: A website developed by the University of Cambridge and the University of Bristol devoted to applications of inoculation theory. It is aimed at students, researchers, and the general public.

https://www.apa.org/monitor/2019/11/cover-politics: A cover story at the American Psychological Association webpage discussing the pertinence of political psychology for understanding current democratic challenges as well as some practical applications to improve democracy.

https://www.getbadnews.com/en: Have a chance to play the Bad News game.

References

Adida, C. L., Lo, A., & Platas, M. R. (2018). Perspective taking can promote short-term inclusionary behavior toward Syrian refugees. *Proceedings of the National Academy of Sciences*, *115* (38), 9521–9526.

Asch, S. E. (1951). Effects of group pressure upon the modification and distortion of judgments. In H. Guetzkow (Ed.), *Groups, leadership and men; research in human relations* (pp. 177–190). Pittsburgh: Carnegie Press.

Badrinathan, S., Chauchard, S., & Siddiqui, N. (2025). Misinformation and support for vigilantism: An experiment in India and Pakistan. *American Political Science Review*, *119* (2), 947–965.

Bergman, M., & Fernández, P. (2024). Affective polarization in Latin America: A research note. *Latin American Politics and Society*, *67*, 114–132.

Blais, A. (2006). What affects voter turnout? *Annual Review of Political Science*, *9* (1), 111–125.

Bond, R. M., Fariss, C. J., Jones, J. J., Kramer, A. D., Marlow, C., Settle, J. E., & Fowler, J. H. (2012). A 61-million-person experiment in social influence and political mobilization. *Nature*, *489* (7415), 295–298.

Broockman, D., & Kalla, J. (2016). Durably reducing transphobia: A field experiment on door-to-door canvassing. *Science*, *352* (6282), 220–224.

Gerber, A. S., & Rogers, T. (2009). Descriptive social norms and motivation to vote: Everybody's voting and so should you. *The Journal of Politics*, *71* (1), 178–191.

Goodwin, T. (2012). Why we should reject 'nudge'. *Politics*, *32* (2), 85–92.

Green, D. P., Wilke, A. M., & Cooper, J. (2020). Countering violence against women by encouraging disclosure: A mass media experiment in rural Uganda. *Comparative Political Studies*, *53* (14), 2283–2320.

Hallsworth, M., List, J. A., Metcalfe, R. D., & Vlaev, I. (2017). The behavioralist as tax collector: Using natural field experiments to enhance tax compliance. *Journal of Public Economics*, *148*, 14–31.

Larson, J. M., & Lewis, J. I. (2025). Reducing prejudice toward refugees: Evidence that social networks influence attitude change in Uganda. *American Political Science Review*, *119* (1), 349–367.

Levitsky, S., & Ziblatt, D. (2019). *How democracies die.* London: Penguin.

Lewandowsky, S. (2021). Climate change disinformation and how to combat it. *Annual Review of Public Health*, *42* (1), 1–21.

Lewandowsky, S., & Van Der Linden, S. (2021). Countering misinformation and fake news through inoculation and prebunking. *European Review of Social Psychology*, *32* (2), 348–384.

Loomba, S., De Figueiredo, A., Piatek, S. J., De Graaf, K., & Larson, H. J. (2021). Measuring the impact of COVID-19 vaccine misinformation on vaccination intent in the UK and USA. *Nature Human Behaviour*, *5* (3), 337–348.

McGuire, W. J. (1961). Resistance to persuasion conferred by active and passive prior refutation of the same and alternative counterarguments. *The Journal of Abnormal and Social Psychology*, *63* (2), 326.

McGuire, W. J. (1964). Some contemporary approaches. In *Advances in experimental social psychology* (Vol. 1, pp. 191–229). New York: Academic Press.

Miller, J. M., & Krosnick, J. A. (1998). The impact of candidate name order on election outcomes. *Public Opinion Quarterly*, *62* (3), 291–330.

Nord, M., Altman, D., Angiolillo, F., Fernandes, T., Good God, A., & Lindberg, S. I. (2025). *Democracy report 2025: 25 years of autocratization – Democracy trumped?* Gothenburg: University of Gothenburg: V-Dem Institute.

Nyhan, B., Porter, E., Reifler, J., & Wood, T. J. (2020). Taking fact-checks literally but not seriously? The effects of journalistic fact-checking on factual beliefs and candidate favorability. *Political Behavior*, *42*, 939–960.

Roozenbeek, J., & Van der Linden, S. (2019). Fake news game confers psychological resistance against online misinformation. *Palgrave Communications*, *5* (1), 1–10.

Roozenbeek, J., Van Der Linden, S., Goldberg, B., Rathje, S., & Lewandowsky, S. (2022). Psychological inoculation improves resilience against misinformation on social media. *Science Advances, 8* (34), eabo6254.

Sanders, M., Stockdale, E., Hume, S., & John, P. (2021). Loss aversion fails to replicate in the coronavirus pandemic: Evidence from an online experiment. *Economics Letters, 199*, 109433.

Traberg, C. S., Roozenbeek, J., & Van Der Linden, S. (2022). Psychological inoculation against misinformation: Current evidence and future directions. *The ANNALS of the American Academy of Political and Social Science, 700* (1), 136–151.

Van der Linden, S., Leiserowitz, A., Rosenthal, S., & Maibach, E. (2017). Inoculating the public against misinformation about climate change. *Global Challenges, 1* (2), 1600008.

Voelkel, J. G., Ashokkumar, A., Abeles, A. T., Crawford, J. T., Fuller, K., Redekopp, C., … & Willer, R. (2026). A registered report megastudy on the persuasiveness of the most-cited climate messages. *Nature Climate Change, 16,* 214–225.

Voelkel, J. G., Stagnaro, M. N., Chu, J. Y., Pink, S. L., Mernyk, J. S., Redekopp, C., … & Willer, R. (2024). Megastudy testing 25 treatments to reduce antidemocratic attitudes and partisan animosity. *Science, 386*, eadh4764.

Wagner, M. (2024). Affective polarization in Europe. *European Political Science Review, 16* (3), 378–392.

Wolfowicz, M., Weisburd, D., & Hasisi, B. (2022). *Counter-radicalization interventions: A review of the evidence.* Stockholm: Institute for Futures Studies.

Section 5

Key Emerging Areas

Chapter 11

Emerging Areas in Political Psychology

Introduction

Where is political psychology research heading? In this concluding chapter discusses some of the emerging areas and methodologies in the field. It begins by discussing the ongoing expansion of the geographical scope of political psychology research. The rest of this chapter focuses on emerging research areas. It discusses the evolving methodologies used in the area, the increasing dialogue between political psychology and neuroscience, and the use of artificial intelligence as a research tool.

Expanding the Geographical Scope of Research

The development of political psychology has been geographically uneven, with a historically disproportionate focus on the United States and Europe. Expanding the geographical scope to Latin America, Africa, Asia, and the Middle East is increasingly recognized as a key priority among political psychologists (Rivera Pichardo et al., 2022) for two key reasons. First, a discipline that overly focuses on a narrow range of societies that share specific historical patterns, cultural characteristics, and demographic composition cannot make universal claims about the psychology of political behavior. Second, the application of Western theories to non-Western contexts risks offering limited insights for understanding the psychological underpinnings of mass political behavior in those settings (Hawi et al., 2022).

As political psychologists grow more aware of these challenges, there have been systematic efforts to diversify the discipline. For instance, the International Society of Political Psychology has implemented important steps for internationalizing and diversifying the field. A Vice President for Membership, Internationalization and Diversity was appointed in 2016 with the purpose of making political psychology more inclusive and diverse by encouraging collaborations with underrepresented regions and by helping researchers from the Global South overcome financial and practical constraints. The effort to diversify political psychology is beginning to pay off as evidenced by an increased

DOI: 10.4324/9781003460084-16

geographical representation at the International Society of Political Psychology annual meeting (Osborne & Sibley, 2022).

At the same time, more needs to be done, especially when it comes to assessing how well some of the most prevalent findings in the discipline replicate across different contexts. A number of scholars have recently produced important research to fill this gap (see Hawi et al., 2022; Rivera Pichardo et al., 2022 for an overview of different studies). This stream of work finds that while some key political psychology theories (such as contact theory – e.g., Demarest & Langer, 2025; Dzordzormenyoh, 2025) seem to replicate well in non-Western contexts, others – such as psychological differences between liberals and conservatives – seem to depend on the characteristics of the political system of each country (see Beattie et al., 2022). Still, this line of inquiry remains underdeveloped. Research programs investigating political psychology in non-Western countries are much needed, and their number is expected to grow in the future, especially considering the priority given by the political psychology community.

Research on Emerging Societal Challenges

Political psychology aims at understanding the psychological causes of important contemporary sociopolitical phenomena. A large body of recent research investigates growing challenges for liberal democracy, including the rise in outpartisan hostility (e.g., Iyengar et al., 2019), increasing opposition to core democratic principles (Druckman, 2024), the widespread endorsement of conspiracy theories (e.g., Douglas & Sutton, 2025), science and climate change denial (Jylhä et al., 2022), as well as the rise in disruptive and toxic political behavior (Bilewicz & Soral, 2022). By focusing on the psychological underpinnings of such political behaviors, political psychologists uncover new motivations that help interpret them. For example, in investigating why some people willingly disseminate fake news or spread hostile rumors about political opponents, Arceneaux and colleagues identified that these individuals share a **need for chaos** defined as "a desire for a new beginning through the destruction of order and established structures" (Arceneaux et al., 2021, p. 2). Such advances are valuable in understanding the psychological substrates of key political phenomena.

> **Need for chaos**: A psychological motivation characterized by a desire for a new beginning achieved through the destruction of social order and established structures.

Research on the psychological roots of prejudice becomes once more particularly relevant today following the rise of authoritarian candidates globally and the targeting of ethnic, religious, sexual, and gender minorities. This has led to novel theoretical and methodological approaches aimed at describing the contemporary psychological motivations behind prejudice, complementing

Intersectionality: A theoretical perspective that posits that social characteristics such as gender, race, and sexual orientation intersect to create distinct experiences of inequality, stereotyping, and discrimination.

existing frameworks that we discussed in Chapter 6. For instance, research in social and political psychology is increasingly informed by **intersectional** perspectives. Intersectionality posits that to better understand discrimination, researchers should account for the fact that key social characteristics (e.g., gender, race, sexual orientation) intersect, producing distinct patterns of inequality, stereotyping, and discrimination for those located at the intersection (e.g., Black gay women – Cassese, 2019; Hudson et al., 2024). Such frameworks are valuable because they add nuance to the psychological motivations of discrimination. Others investigate how prejudice toward one social group interacts with prejudice toward other groups. In an important study, Turnbull-Dugarte and Ortega (2024) showed that ethnically prejudiced citizens strategically update their attitudes toward LGBTQI members in a positive direction, as a way to disidentify with Muslims. These findings are important for understanding the complexity of prejudice in the 21st century and add nuance to classic studies in the field.

On the other end, there is an emerging stream of research that explores the political psychology of empathy to understand why some people consistently show compassion and stand in solidarity with different minority groups, which is important for reducing interethnic conflict (e.g., Sirin et al., 2021). Other emerging approaches seek to understand how prejudice affects the political behavior and mobilization of stigmatized minorities. For instance, two studies on entirely different populations – first- and second-generation immigrants in France and lesbian, gay, and bisexual citizens in Sweden – found that minority political participation increases when these citizens are surrounded by other minorities (Ahlskog et al., 2026; McAvay & Vasilopoulos, 2024). Given that contemporary societies are becoming increasingly diverse, research on the political psychology of prejudice and minority mobilization is expected to intensify.

Emerging Methodologies and Approaches

Psychophysiological Measures

Political psychology is characterized by strong interdisciplinarity drawing on a scientific toolkit that borrows from many disciplines in the social sciences (e.g., sociology, psychology, political science) and beyond (biology, neuroscience). Political psychologists are making use of technological and scientific advancements to improve our ability to understand the psychological motivations of political behavior. Emerging areas in this direction focus on neuroscience, biology, and large language models. All of these approaches offer the advantage of more objective measures of human activity that do not rely on respondents' assessments of their own behavior. This is important because self-reporting of behavior is subject to biases, such as not accurately recalling one's actions or responding in a way that is deemed socially acceptable.

Facial electromyography (fEMG): A psychophysiological method that measures small, rapid bioelectric signals produced by facial muscle contractions and is used to detect emotional expression.

Researchers increasingly rely on psychophysiological and neural measures of political behavior. These methods are particularly useful for revealing unconscious processes that may underlie political decision-making and are difficult to capture using conventional methods (see Bakker & Schumacher, 2025). For example, one stream of recent research draws on measures using **facial electromyography** (fEMG). fEMG measures "tiny, partially invisible, rapid, bioelectric signals at the surface of the skin that are generated due to muscle contractions in a specific region" (Bakker & Schumacher, 2025, p. 10). It is used to measure whether a person experiences positive or negative emotions. For instance, in a series of carefully designed experiments, a sample of participants was connected to fEMG equipment and shown short news clips about different topics, such as immigration or climate change from a left-wing or right-wing angle (Bakker et al., 2021). The allocation of messages was decided at random. The researchers discovered that while being shown messages from one's own ideological camp did not increase positive affect, exposure to messages from the opposing ideological camp evoked negative affect. This is an important finding showing that exposure to political discourse yields physiological responses among citizens.

Neurobiological Mechanisms

As we discovered throughout this volume a key hypothesis of political psychology research is that our political attitudes and beliefs stem from deep-seated and largely unconscious mechanisms. This was for instance the overarching theoretical framework of some of the earliest studies in the field (e.g., Fromm, 1941). Research drawing on neurobiological mechanisms shares this assumption. Yet, instead of relying on psychoanalytic methods to reveal the unconscious drives of our political behavior, it focuses on brain structure and functions with the intent to uncover how these are associated with political decision-making. Specifically, political neuroscientists seek to explain political behavior by studying the tissue structure of the brain using Magnetic Resonance Imaging, a non-invasive technique that uses magnetic fields and radio waves to produce high-resolution brain images.

Much of political psychology research drawing on neuroscientific methods has focused on the association between the amygdalae and political orientations. The amygdalae are structures in the brain consisting of two parts,

System justification: A psychological tendency to view the social and political system on which one depends as fair, legitimate, and desirable.

one in each brain hemisphere, that govern appraisals of threat and (mostly) negative emotion processing. The amygdala's role is to "keep us grounded in our environment by orienting us toward objects warranting further inspection and alerting us to their aversive or appetitive status" (Panish & Nam, 2024, p. 5). Studies have found that the amygdala size and structure are associated with political orientations. Specifically, the size of the right amygdala has been associated with political conservatism and **system justification,** or in other words, a psychological tendency to view the social and political system that one depends on as fair and legitimate (Nam, 2020; Zmigrod, 2025). However, the causal mechanism behind this association is not entirely clear. As Zmigrod argues, one explanation is that people with enlarged amygdalae are more sensitive to threat and hence gravitate toward conservatism as an ideology that helps minimize threat (2025, see also Chapters 3 and 4 in this book). Another explanation is that endorsing specific ideologies may in fact change our brains through mechanisms such as media information consumption. In Zmigrod's words, "the experience of being immersed in conservative, system-justifying ideologies [is] an experience that alters our emotional biochemistry in a way that leads to structural brain changes" (2025, p. 201).

Artificial Intelligence (AI) and Large Language Models

The rise of AI is bringing fundamental societal change and potentially entails serious economic, social, and political risks. Still, due to AI's ability to analyze and organize very large volumes of data, it is also immensely useful for conducting scientific research. The use of AI in political psychology is in its infancy, yet it is expected to develop significantly in the following years (Shugars & Argyle, 2025). **Large language models (LLMs),** such as ChatGPT, Claude, or Gemini, are particularly relevant for political psychology. LLMs are a subset of AI focusing on comprehending and processing human language. They have several applications in political psychology research (see Yu et al., 2025). For instance, rather than relying on traditional surveys and laboratory experiments, LLMs can analyze very large quantities of unstructured data such as social media posts to investigate how people reason about their political choices (Yu et al., 2025). This can be particularly useful for

Large language model (LLM): A type of artificial intelligence designed to comprehend and process human language. In political psychology, large language models are used to analyze large amounts of unstructured text data.

uncovering psychological processes that contribute to attitudes based on people's own words rather than pre-designed questionnaires. Such approaches are valuable in understanding phenomena such as climate change denial or vaccine hesitancy (Yu et al., 2025).

Another promising application of LLMs in political psychology concerns combating misinformation. As we stressed in the previous chapter, the proliferation of misinformation has a broad range of deleterious societal and political consequences, from undermining democracy to endangering public health. Countering misinformation has been proven a particularly challenging task as people exposed are unlikely to update their beliefs even when they are shown that they were victims of misinformation (Nyhan & Reifler, 2010). Researchers have proposed that a more effective approach could involve LLM-generated responses. Even though LLMs can themselves be used for disseminating misinformation, they could also be effectively deployed to counter it through corrections, which are tailored to the psychological and demographic profile of each independent user (Proma et al., 2025). Such personalized interventions are deemed more effective compared to non-tailored methods, yet their large-scale application involves ethical risks as they could be used by malevolent actors (Proma et al., 2025). However, the use of AI in political psychology either as a research or communication tool is expected to intensify in the next few years.

Conclusion

This chapter identified three key emerging directions in which political psychology is expected to head in the future. The first concerns the need to diversify political psychology research by developing hypotheses and testing established findings, outside of the familiar terrains of the United States and Europe. The second involves the continuous scientific need to make theoretical advances for understanding a complex and evolving political world. Finally, future political psychology can rely on technology that allows for an array of methodological choices that were not available until recent years. All of these areas provide optimism for the future of the discipline and pave the way for a more nuanced, robust, and inclusive political psychology.

Further Reading

Busby, E. C., Karpowitz, C. F., & C. J. Wong (Eds.). *Handbook of innovations in political psychology*. Cheltenham: Edward Elgar. An edited volume devoted on emerging research themes in political psychology.

Zmigrod, L. (2025). *The ideological brain*. London: Penguin. A fascinating and accessible book drawing on neuroscience to uncover the connections between brain biology and political ideology.

References

Adorno, T. W., Frenkel-Brunswik, E., Levinson, D. J., & Nevitt Sanford, R. (1950). *The authoritarian personality*. New York: Harper & Row.

Ahlskog, R., Grahn, M., & Turnbull-Dugarte, S. J. (2026). Rallied by thy neighbor: How minority spatial concentration increases voter turnout. *Journal of Politics*, in print.

Arceneaux, K., Gravelle, T. B., Osmundsen, M., Petersen, M. B., Reifler, J., & Scotto, T. J. (2021). Some people just want to watch the world burn: the prevalence, psychology and politics of the 'Need for Chaos'. *Philosophical Transactions of the Royal Society B*, *376* (1822), 20200147.

Bakker, B. N., & Schumacher, G. (2025). Using measures of psychophysiological and neural activity to advance understanding of psychological processes in politics. In E. C. Busby, C. F. Karpowitz, & C. J. Wong (Eds.), *Handbook of innovations in political psychology* (pp. 415–452). Cheltenham: Edward Elgar Publishing.

Bakker, B. N., Schumacher, G., & Rooduijn, M. (2021). Hot politics? Affective responses to political rhetoric. *American Political Science Review*, *115* (1), 150–164.

Beattie, P., Chen, R., & Bettache, K. (2022). When left is right and right is left: The psychological correlates of political ideology in China. *Political Psychology*, *43* (3), 457–488.

Bilewicz, M., & Soral, W. (2022). The politics of hate: Derogatory language in politics and intergroup relations. In D. Osborne & C. G. Sibley (Eds.), *The Cambridge handbook of political psychology* (pp. 429–441). Cambridge: Cambridge University Press.

Cassese, E. C. (2019). Intersectional stereotyping in political decision making. In *Oxford research encyclopedia of politics* (pp. 1–27). Oxford: Oxford University Press

Demarest, L., & Langer, A. (2025). Ethnic diversity and intergroup relations among Nigerian adolescents: Testing intergroup contact and political deliberation theories. *International Journal of Intercultural Relations*, *105*, 102149.

Douglas, K. M., & Sutton, R. M. (2025). The social psychology of conspiracy theories: Key insights and future challenges. In B. Gawronski (Ed.), *Advances in experimental social psychology* (Vol. 71, pp. 1–68). London: Academic Press.

Druckman, J. N. (2024). How to study democratic backsliding. *Political Psychology*, *45*, 3–42.

Dzordzormenyoh, M. K. (2025). Predictors of immigrant acceptance in Africa: A multi-sample analysis of contact hypothesis and neighbourhood violence. *International Migration*, *63* (4), e70055.

Fromm, E. (1941). *Escape from freedom*. New York: Avon Books.

Hawi, D., Bou Zeineddine, F., Saab, R., Ayanian, A. H., & Harb, C. (2022). Political psychology in the Arab region: A commentary on navigating research in unstable contexts. In D. Osborne & C. G. Sibley (Eds.), *The Cambridge handbook of political psychology* (pp. 624–639). Cambridge: Cambridge University Press.

Hudson, S. K. T. J., Myer, A., & Berney, E. C. (2024). Stereotyping, prejudice, and discrimination at the intersection of race and gender: An intersectional theory primer. *Social and Personality Psychology Compass*, *18* (2), e12939.

Iyengar, S., Lelkes, Y., Levendusky, M., Malhotra, N., & Westwood, S. J. (2019). The origins and consequences of affective polarization in the United States. *Annual Review of Political Science*, *22* (1), 129–146.

Jylhä, K. M., Stanley, S. K., Ojala, M., & Clarke, E. J. (2022). Science denial. *European Psychologist, 28* (3), 151–161.

McAvay, H., & Vasilopoulos, P. (2024). Do neighborhoods empower or disenfranchise? Coethnic concentration, spatial disadvantage, and voter registration in France. *The Journal of Politics, 86* (4), 1277–1290.

Nam, H. H. (2020). Neuroscientific approaches to the study of system justification. *Current Opinion in Behavioral Sciences, 34*, 205–210.

Nyhan, B., & Reifler, J. (2010). When corrections fail: The persistence of political misperceptions. *Political Behavior, 32* (2), 303–330.

Osborne, D., & Sibley, C. G. (2022). Advancing an international perspective on the psychology of political behaviour. In D. Osborne, & C. G. Sibley (Eds.), *The Cambridge handbook of political psychology* (pp. 3–21). Cambridge: Cambridge University Press.

Panish, A., & Nam, H. H. (2024). The neurobiology of political ideology: Theories, findings, and future directions. *Social and Personality Psychology Compass, 18* (1), e12916.

Proma, A., Pate, N., Druckman, J., Ghoshal, G., & Hoque, E. (2025, June). Personalizing LLM responses to combat political misinformation. In *Proceedings of the 33rd ACM conference on user modeling, adaptation and personalization* (pp. 134–143).

Rivera Pichardo, E. J., Vargas Salfate, S., & Jost, J. T. (2022). Political psychology in the global South. In D. Osborne & C. G. Sibley (Eds.), *The Cambridge handbook of political psychology* (pp. 601–623). Cambridge: Cambridge University Press.

Sirin, C. V., Valentino, N. A., & Villalobos, J. D. (2021). *Seeing us in them: Social divisions and the politics of group empathy*. Cambridge: Cambridge University Press.

Shugars, S., & Argyle, L. P. (2025). Computational political psychology. In E. C. Busby, C. F. Karpowitz, & C. J. Wong (Eds.), *Handbook of innovations in political psychology* (pp. 492–512). Cheltenham: Edward Elgar Publishing.

Turnbull-Dugarte, S. J., & Ortega, A. L. (2024). Instrumentally inclusive: The political psychology of homonationalism. *American Political Science Review, 118* (3), 1360–1378.

Yu, D., Thompson, B. D., & Dubey, R. (2025). Leveraging AI to advance psychological research for climate policy. *Current Opinion in Behavioral Sciences, 65*, 101547.

Zmigrod, L. (2025). *The ideological brain*. London: Penguin.

Index

Note: **Bold** page numbers refer to tables.

For Product Safety Concerns and Information please contact our EU representative GPSR@taylorandfrancis.com
Taylor & Francis Verlag GmbH, Kaufingerstraße 24, 80331 München, Germany

www.ingramcontent.com/pod-product-compliance
Lightning Source LLC
LaVergne TN
LVHW020847180926
848329LV00027B/295
9781032606675